A Mexican-American Family of California:

In the Service of Three Flags

John P. Schmal and Jennifer Vo

HERITAGE BOOKS
2007

HERITAGE BOOKS
AN IMPRINT OF HERITAGE BOOKS, INC.

Books, CDs, and more—Worldwide

For our listing of thousands of titles see our website at
www.HeritageBooks.com

Published 2007 by
HERITAGE BOOKS, INC.
Publishing Division
65 East Main Street
Westminster, Maryland 21157-5026

Copyright © 2003 John P. Schmal and Jennifer Vo

Other books by John Schmal:
Naturalizations of Mexican Americans: Extracts Volumes 1–4
The Journey to Latino Political Representation

Other books by John Schmal and Donna Morales:
Mexican-American Genealogical Research: Following the Paper Trail to Mexico
The Dominguez Family: A Mexican-American Journey
The Indigenous Roots of a Mexican-American Family

All rights reserved. No part of this book may be reproduced or transmitted in any form or by any means, electronic or mechanical, including photocopying, recording or by any information storage and retrieval system without written permission from the author, except for the inclusion of brief quotations in a review.

International Standard Book Number: 978-0-7884-2448-9

Dora Melendez Basulto (Grandmother of Jennifer Vo)

DEDICATION:

This work is dedicated to the two most important women in my life:

My mother:

Sarah Basulto Evans

And my grandmother:

Dora Melendez Basulto

TABLE OF CONTENTS

TITLE PAGE
PHOTOGRAPH
DEDICATION
PREFACE
ACKNOWLEDGEMENTS

INTRODUCTION	1
SPAIN	7
The Cultural Dimension	7
Early Spain	7
The German Kingdom	11
The Islamic Interlude	13
The Era of Conquest	15
Decline	17
THE ORIGIN OF MY PEOPLE	21
Indigenous Roots	21
Beringia	22
Migrations	23
Cultural Diffusions	26
THE INDIANS OF MEXICO	31
Agriculture	31
The Diversity of Mexico	33
The Olmecs	36
The Zapotecs and Mayas	36
The Valley of Mexico	38
The Toltecs	41
The Mexica	41
The Aztec Empire	44

TABLE OF CONTENTS

INDIGENOUS MEXICAN ROOTS — 47
- La Madre Patria: Sinaloa y Sonora — 47
- The First Contact (1531) — 49
- Epidemic Disease — 52
- Distant Enclave — 53
- The Mayo and Yaqui Indians — 55
- The Apache Threat — 60

SINALOA AND SONORA — 65
- Sonora — 65
- Álamos — 66
- Sinaloa — 68
- Rosario — 69
- El Fuerte — 70
- One Step Up the Social Ladder — 71

ALTA CALIFORNIA — 75
- Early Expeditions — 75
- Foreign Threats — 76

SPANISH COLONIAL INSTITUTIONS — 79
- Missions, Presidios, and Pueblos — 79
- The Mission — 80
- The Presidio — 84
- The Pueblo — 86
- Los Soldados de Cuera — 87

THE FOUNDING OF SAN DIEGO — 95
- The Expeditions of 1769 — 95
- San Diego — 97
- Felipe de Neve — 98

THE EXPEDITION OF 1781 — 101
- The Search for Recruits — 101
- The Expedition — 104

TABLE OF CONTENTS

THE FOUNDING OF LOS ANGELES — 109
   The Founding of Los Angeles — 109

SANTA BARBARA — 117
   Santa Barbara — 117

THE RELUCTANT SETTLERS — 133
   Luis Quintero — 133

THE CALIFORNIA SOLDIERS — 141
   Pedro Gabriel Valenzuela — 141
   Juan Matias Olivas — 148
   José Rosalino Fernandez — 155

THE FELIZ FAMILY — 161
   Anastacio María Feliz — 161

FROM SPANISH TO MEXICAN — 167
   José Pablo Olivas — 167
   Upheaval — 170
   Independence from Spain — 171
   Antonio María Valenzuela — 173

THE CHANGING OF THE GUARD — 175
   A Soldier of the Republic — 175
   James K. Polk and California — 178
   The Mexican-American War — 180
   The Treaty of Guadalupe Hidalgo — 181
   María Antonia Olivas de Esquivel — 183

TABLE OF CONTENTS

THE ORTEGA FAMILY — 187
  An American Citizen — 187
  Gregorio Ortega — 189
  Valentine Ortega and Theodora Tapia — 192
  Isabel Ortega and Refugio Gonzalez
    Melendez — 196

IN THE SERVICE OF THEIR COUNTRY — 201
  Mexican-American Contributions to
    Freedom — 201
  The Korean War — 204
  Vietnam — 206

THE LATER GENERATIONS — 209
  Theodora Ortega Melendez — 209
  Sarah Basulto — 211

AN AMERICAN EXPERIENCE — 215
  Jennifer Kunkel Vo — 215
  The Next Generation — 218

BIBLIOGRAPHY — 221

INDEX — 234

PREFACE
By John P. Schmal

I have been friends with Jennifer Vo since 1995. She is one of the nicest human beings I've ever known and her mother and grandmother are equally nice people. Because I have been doing genealogical and historical research on Mexican American families for a number of years, I took an interest in the fact that Jennifer and her family were well aware that their family had been living in California for many generations.

But it is interesting that the family actually did not know the details or the names of their earliest ancestors in California. They had always known and felt that California had been their land for many generations. This was the oral tradition that was carried down through 12 generations and at least 215 years.

I proceeded to track down Jennifer's ancestry and was very pleased to find that their family's long journey through California history was not only real but that it was very well documented. All I had to do was check the mission records for Santa Barbara, San Buenaventura, and San Gabriel.

Millions of people live in the greater Los Angeles area, but the vast majority of us have ancestors from other states or other countries. But not Jennifer. Her family has been here for a long time. Because of this, California is for Jennifer and her family a very special place.

ACKNOWLEDGEMENTS

We gratefully acknowledge the contributions and assistance of the following: the Los Angeles Family History Center, the Santa Monica Public Library, Sarah Basulto Evans, Dora Basulto, Eva Aubert, the Santa Barbara Mission Archives, the *Southern California Quarterly*, the Santa Barbara Trust for Historical Preservation, the Ventura County Historical Society, Lillian Ramos Wold, Mimi Lozano, and the Family of Simon Melendez.

We most gratefully acknowledge the permission we received from many authors and publishing companies to use certain quotes as a means of enhancing our story. We also give thanks to both Eddie Martinez and Kirk Bowen for their graphics contributions.

Finally, we give great thanks to Bob Lopez, one of the organizers of *Los Pobladores*, who offered his assistance in helping us put together the loose ends of this great epic story. Bob is a fellow descendant of the founding fathers and mothers of the Pueblo of Los Angeles.

INTRODUCTION

It has been said that in order to really know ourselves we need to learn about our ancestors. In so doing, we can see that the decisions made by those who came before us have repercussions which encompass our very existence today. When studying the conduct of our forebears, we become witnesses to their accomplishments and – in the process – may become cognizant of our own potential as human beings.

Throughout history, the migration of humans from one land to another has had enormous consequences. Our nation was forged from just such migratory forces. And yet, we may not fully appreciate the difficulties and risks that the journeys entailed. These journeys become even more significant when we can gain insight into the opportunities and dangers faced by our forebears.

In an America where almost everyone looks to a faraway land as their ancestral homeland, it is unusual – indeed rare – to find anyone who can boast that their ancestors stayed in one place for many generations. The farther west you go in the United States, the more this seems to be true. One very profound exception to this rule is my family.

My name is Jennifer Vo and I am both a Mexican American and an eleventh-generation Californian. Like millions of other Californians I was born and raised in the Los Angeles area. But when I drive to work each morning, I pass by a small street sign that states "City of Los Angeles: Established 1781."

While this sign may not catch the attention of most commuters, I smile as I pass it by. The reason that I smile is because I know

INTRODUCTION

that my ancestors were there at the founding of *El Pueblo de Nuestra la Reina de Los Angeles del Rio Porcioncula* on September 4, 1781.

In the last half of the Eighteenth Century, many of my ancestors were impoverished citizens from Sinaloa and Sonora, two northwestern provinces of Mexico, located along the Gulf of California. In 1774, King Carlos III of Spain had authorized the settlement of the California communities we call San Gabriel, Los Angeles, and Santa Barbara. He believed that the establishment of pueblos, missions and presidios in these areas would serve as a bulwark against the looming threat of the Russian and British empires, both of which were moving closer to California.

Recruited from the poorest classes of Sinaloa and Sonora, my family played a pivotal role in this settlement. Several of my ancestors came to California in the famous *Expedition of 1781*. Some came as soldados (soldiers), while others came as pobladores (settlers). Although they served under the flag of the Spanish Empire, they were natives of Mexico and so were almost all of their fellow soldados and pobladores.

This small pueblo (which we now call Los Angeles) would eventually form the nucleus of a thriving multi-ethnic, multicultural urban center with a population of almost 10 million people. After the founding of Los Angeles, many of my ancestors moved on and played an even more vital role in the founding of *El Presidio de Santa Barbara* on April 21, 1782.

INTRODUCTION

The majority of my ancestors in this period belonged to a unique breed of Spanish soldiers called *los soldados de cuera* (the leather-jacket soldiers). Prepared to serve and perhaps die in the service of the Spanish Empire, these young men from northern Mexico took their families with them to this strange, untamed land, uncertain of the challenges that lay ahead. However, with the challenges and uncertainty came great opportunities and we are certain that they were well aware of this.

In an attempt to understand the many forces at work in the cultural, historical, and genealogical development of my family, we have broadened the scope of this study to include significant events and movements that took place in both Europe and the Americas many years before my ancestors stepped foot on the soil of Southern California. For this reason, a brief history of Spain and a description of the Native American migrations have been included.

In my family, twelve generations of Californians have served under three flags: as soldiers, tailors, farmers, laborers, machinists, editors, quality assurance managers, and domestic engineers. In the final analysis, we are able to witness through the eyes of one family the evolution of California from a Spanish province to a Mexican state. And, when California – in 1850 – became the thirty-first state of the United States, my family was there.

California
The Golden State, as California is so frequently called, needs no introduction. Located on the western coast of North America with a total land area of 155,973 square miles, California has a long

INTRODUCTION

mountainous coastline with a central valley running through the middle of the state. The Sierra Nevada Mountains run through a significant portion of the eastern state.

Today, California is the most populous state of the Union and boasts the fifth largest economy in the world. But two hundred years ago, as a Spanish province, California had a total Hispanic population of only 1,500,[1] surrounded by a multitude of Native American tribes that probably numbered about 150,000.

The Spanish colonial administrators of the Eighteenth Century saw California (which they called *Alta California – Upper California*) as the northern extension of *Baja California – Lower California*. Although the Spaniards had discovered Baja California soon after the conquest of central Mexico, the 800-mile-long peninsula presented a formidable barrier to northward travel. Not until 1697 did the Spaniards finally establish a permanent settlement at Loreto on the Baja Peninsula. In the century that followed, this small outpost would serve as a base for the exploration of Alta California.

The origin of the name California has never been resolved with any certainty. The best guess suggested by several historians is that California was derived from two Latin words *Calida fornax* (hot furnace). Climatic conditions in the southern part of Baja California when the Spaniards arrived in the Sixteenth Century

---

[1] Carolyn Gale McGovern, "Hispanic Population in Alta California" (Unpublished Master's Thesis, California State University, Northridge, 1978), p. 154.

INTRODUCTION

may very well have reminded Hernan Cortés and the other Spanish explorers of a heated furnace. In addition, the Catalan word *Californo* means "hot oven."[2]

However, the California historian, Charles E. Chapman, wrote that the Spanish explorers – as a rule – did not assign Latin names to the lands they discovered. He stated that "a more likely suggestion was that the Spaniards might have misunderstood some Indian word and applied it as a name." Probably the most interesting suggestion is a reference to an old Spanish novel entitled *Las sergas de Esplandián* (The Deeds of Esplandián), which referred to a strange and romantic island called *California*. The publication of this book is believed to have taken place in the late 1400s and its re-issues (1519, 1521, 1525, and 1526) were in years contemporaneous with Cortéz' early activities in New Spain. The fact that Baja California was originally thought to be an island lends some credence to this theory.[3]

Although Spain had claimed Alta California as her sovereign territory as early as 1542, her vast diversified interests in other areas of the Western Hemisphere kept her preoccupied for two centuries. However, by 1769 – when Spain began to send expeditions into Alta California – the Spanish Empire had been in decline for some time. On the other hand, the power and strength of the British, French, and Russian empires had increased

---

[2] Charles E. Chapman, *A History of California: The Spanish Period* (New York: The MacMillan Company, 1921), pp. 55-56.

[3] *Ibid.*, pp. 56-62.

INTRODUCTION

substantially. It was the fear of their encroachment into California or – worse yet – into the silver mines of northwestern Nueva España that prompted the settlement of Alta California.

It is against this backdrop that we witness the entry of four *soldados de cuera* – Juan Matias Olivas, José Rosalino Fernández, Pedro Gabriel Valenzuela, and Anastasio María Feliz – into the pages of California history. In addition, we also witness the reluctant journey of Luis Quintero and his family to Los Angeles, where they represented one of the first eleven founding families of the Pueblo of Los Angeles. All five of these men and their families are my ancestors and it is because of their tenacity and endurance that my family has been an eye-witness to California history for more than two centuries.

SPAIN

> *Politically, Spain was possibly the best equipped of the budding European nations to acquire and control a colonial empire. For approximately six centuries it had been occupied with the expulsion of the non-Christian Moslems (La Reconquista). During this period it had built up the machinery to conquer, control, and exploit. This process resulted in the territorial unification of Spain as well as in the development of an absolute form of government, culminating in the strong Machiavellian rule of Los Reyes Católicos, Ferdinand and Isabella. Their marriage in 1469 led to the creation of a nation-state, Spain.*[1]

The Cultural Dimension

For at least two centuries, the predominant culture influencing the course and direction of my family history was the Hispanic culture. Although the blood of the Native Americans coursed through our veins, Spanish was the mother tongue of my pioneer ancestors who left Sinaloa and Sonora to settle in Alta California. In addition, the early settlers wholeheartedly embraced the Roman Catholic faith which the Spaniards had brought with them from Europe.

Early Spain

A study of Spain's history is a prerequisite to an understanding of

---

[1] Clifford A. Hauberg, *Puerto Rico and the Puerto Ricans* (New York: Twayne Publishers, Inc., 1974), p. 14.

SPAIN

the settlement and conquest of both Mexico and California. The evolution of the Iberian Peninsula from a Roman province to a German kingdom, thence to an Islamic nation, and finally to the Spanish "nation-state," generated the special conditions which gave rise to Spain's era of conquest.

Isolated from the rest of Europe by the snow-capped Pyrenees Mountains, Spain's physical geography has given rise to Spain's own unique role in history. Spain has an area of 297,975 square miles and covers about four-fifths of the Iberian Peninsula, which juts out into the Atlantic. On the following page, we have reproduced a map showing the primary provincial divisions in Spain.[2]

Many kinds of people have conquered and lived in Spain, each group contributing to its traditions and customs. Three thousand years ago, the ancient Phoenicians established colonies in the land now called *España*. Cádiz, believed to be the oldest city in Europe, was founded in 1130 B.C. Starting in 480 B.C., the Carthaginians of Africa conquered and ruled over much of Spain as a colony. During the Second Punic War (218-201 B.C.), the Romans drove the Carthaginians out of Spain. Roman legions

---

[2] J.H. Elliott, *The Spanish World: Civilization and Empire, Europe and the Americas, Past and Present* (New York: Harry N. Abrams, Inc. 1991).

SPAIN

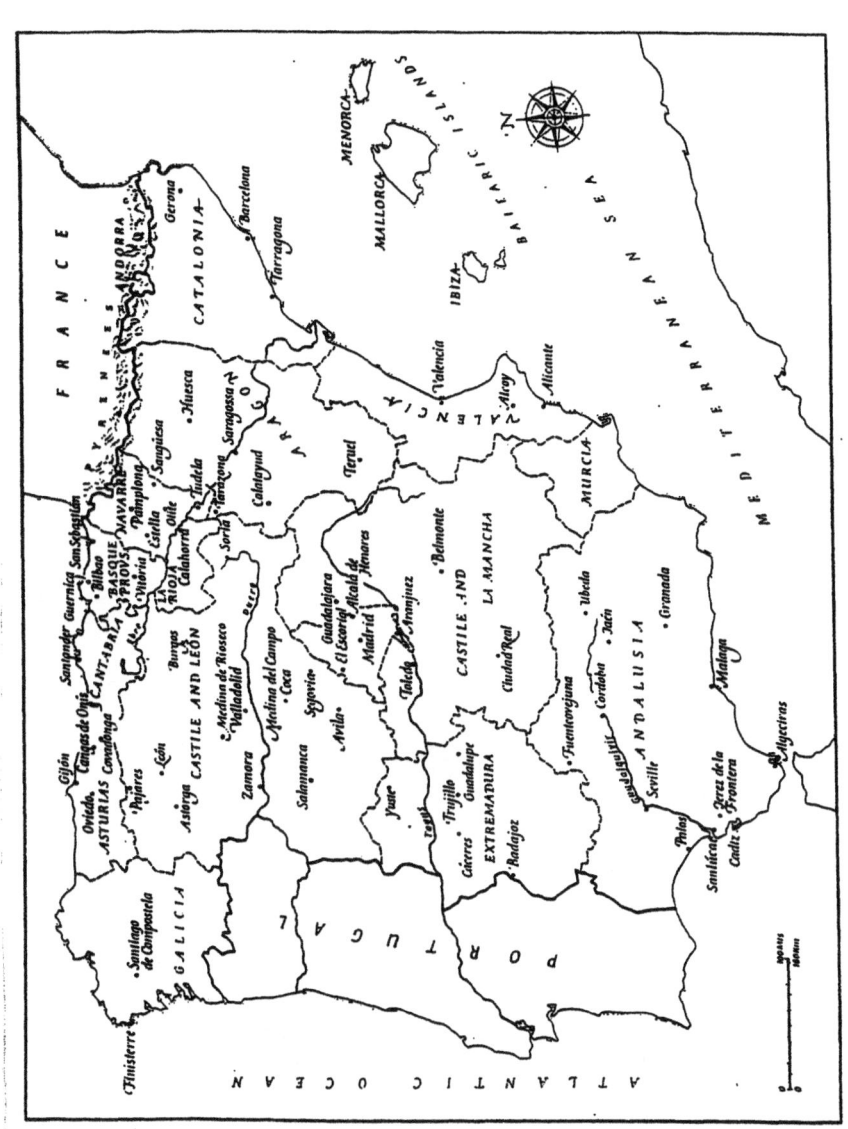

Map of Spain

SPAIN

conquered the whole area (which they called *Hispania*) and stationed garrisons throughout the peninsula. Hispania became the first overseas colony of the Roman Empire.

Although great Roman cities were developed and many Romans made the Iberian Peninsula their home, the natives of Hispania were rebellious and became a continuing source of trouble to the Romans. The Romans respected the Spaniards as "the least amenable of native races," and referred to them "as hard fighters, regardless of pain, and faithful to their leaders and their independence unto death."[3]

The German Kingdom

In the following centuries, as Rome's power declined, fierce German tribes swept into Spain. Sometime around 400 A.D., three powerful German tribes crossed the northern mountain passes. Two of these tribes, the *Suevi* from Germany and the *Alans* from southern Russia, conquered and settled Galicia and Portugal. In the meantime, King Gunderic led his *Vandals* down into central and southern Spain. The Vandals named their southerly kingdom *Vandalusia*, and this area is still called *Andalusia* today.

---

[3] William C. Atkinson, *Spain: A Brief History* (Methuen & Co., Ltd., 1934), p. 6.

SPAIN

Starting in 414, the German chieftain Theodoric led a powerful invasion of Spain. His tribe, the *Visigoths*, had spent two centuries wandering from Scandinavia to the Black Sea, then westward into the Roman Empire. By this time, they had been converted to Christianity and even possessed the Bible in their own tongue.

At first allies of the Romans, the Visigoths conquered the Alans and drove the Vandals across the Straits to North Africa in 429. In the meantime, they confined the Suevians to Galicia. In 456, the Visigoths renounced their alliance with the Romans and commenced with their own occupation of the peninsula. The western portion of the Roman Empire itself crumbled quickly and totally disintegrated in 476.[4]

By 573, the Visigoths had conquered the entire peninsula. However, the kingdom began to founder and was overwhelmed by a new threat: the Moors of Africa. In 711, an Arab leader, with a force of 12,000, landed on the promontory that still bears his name (Gebel-al-Tarik, Gibraltar), and advanced to meet Roderic,

---

[4] *Ibid.*, p. 19.

SPAIN

the last of the Visigoth kings. The Arabs were victorious and further victories in the next year cost Roderic his life and led, within seven years, to the total collapse of the Visigoth kingdom.[5] Thus, Spain next became a Moslem country, except for the tiny northern Visigoth kingdoms of Aragon, Castile, Galicia, Leon, Murcia, and Navarre, all of which remained Christian.

The Islamic Interlude

The Moslems who ruled over most of Spain for the next eight centuries were numerically inferior to the conquered race and chose to be tolerant. Christians who submitted, known as *Mozárabes* (Would-be-Arabs), were allowed to retain their lands, their language, their laws, and their religion.[6]

The Moslem Moors, more culturally advanced than most of the people of feudal Europe, developed a powerful Islamic civilization, unified initially, but later fragmented into smaller, warring kingdoms. The Moors introduced an efficient irrigation system that is still used today. The Moorish arch was introduced

---

[5] *Ibid.*, pp. 20-28.

[6] *Ibid.*, p. 29.

SPAIN

into Spanish architecture, and great Moorish cities were built at Cordoba, Toledo, and Valencia.

Starting with the defeat of the Muslims at the Battle of Covadonga in 718, the small Christian kingdoms of the Iberian Peninsula joined together in fighting the Moors. During the next four centuries, the Christian *Reconquista (Reconquest)* of the Iberian Peninsula was, at best, erratic as the small kingdoms became embroiled in dynastic and territorial squabbles with one another. By 1276, the Moorish kingdom in the peninsula had been whittled down to the southern state of Granada.

On the other hand, the Catholic kingdoms of Castile and Aragon became the two most powerful entities in the Peninsula. In 1469, Prince Ferdinand of Aragon married Queen Isabella of Castile. After the death of Ferdinand's father, the King of Aragon, in 1479, Castile and Aragon were united as a single Christian kingdom. In time, the other smaller kingdoms in the peninsula would be brought into the union.

However, even today, Spain is not an integrated country, but a confederation of regions, many of which have a desire for autonomy. The sense of national identity has always been weak. For many centuries, the peninsula was called "the Spains" and

SPAIN

was composed of separate and distinct realms – Aragon, Leon, Asturias, Catalonia, Valencia, Saragossa, Castile, Toledo, and more.

However, all Spaniards were united in their resentment of the Moors. The determination of Ferdinand and Isabella to make Spain a wholly Catholic country led to the Spanish Inquisition in 1480. The Inquisition hunted down and imprisoned persons who were suspected of not believing Roman Catholic doctrine. Jews and Moslems were treated most harshly. The Jews who did not convert were driven out of Spain, and in 1492, Spanish troops defeated the Moors at Granada, evicting the Moslems entirely from the peninsula.

The Era of Conquest

Having successfully completed the *Reconquista* in 1492, Spain looked for the opportunity to continue its expansion. However, with a solid Muslim wall to the south (in North Africa) and the powerful French kingdom on its northern border, the only direction that Spain could look to was the western sea.

Starting with the voyage of Christopher Columbus in 1492, Spanish explorers set off to find new horizons. In the next half century, the Spaniards would confront many indigenous peoples

SPAIN

in the Western Hemisphere. In every instance, they sought to conquer and then to Christianize. By the middle of the Sixteenth Century, the Spanish Empire comprised most of South America (excluding Brazil), large parts of North America and the Caribbean, as well as the Philippines and smaller areas of Africa.

While many members of the Spanish clergy saw these new conquests as opportunities to Christianize heathens, other members of Spanish society set forth more earthly objectives. Certain parts of the Americas contained great mineral wealth, in particular large amounts of gold and silver ore. Reports of opulent Indian empires reached Spanish shores and galvanized a whole generation of explorers in a search for the newly found riches.

However, Spain's glory was short-lived. In 1588, King Philip II launched his great Spanish Armada in an attempt to bring England to her knees. Wild storms and English guns wiped out a large part of the Armada. Of 131 ships and 25,000 men, 66 ships and 15,000 men never returned.[7] By 1600, Spain's naval supremacy had been overtaken and surpassed by France, Britain, and Holland.

---

[7] *Ibid.*, p. 107.

SPAIN

Decline

The reasons for the decline of Spanish economic power were many and varied. One element in the decline involved the costs of maintaining the vast Spanish empire, which proved crippling over the long term. The immigration of countless Spaniards overseas during the Sixteenth and Seventeenth centuries had caused population growth in Spain to stagnate. This led to sharp increases in labor costs. In addition, the great boon of gold, silver, and gems had flooded Europe and eventually produced rampant inflation. As prices and wages rose, Spanish products became too expensive to compete in other European markets.

Over time, economic realities set in and Spain, which manufactured very little that her European neighbors needed, became dependent upon France, England, and Holland for their manufactured goods. In the meantime, some of the silver mines of the Western Hemisphere had stopped yielding, while Spanish galleons were ruthlessly attacked by French, Dutch, and English pirates on the high seas.

Another factor in Spain's decline was her almost continuous

SPAIN

involvement in the religious and dynastic wars of the Sixteenth and Seventeenth centuries. The religious wars against the Protestants and the Turks and the ongoing struggle with France created a serious drain on Spain's manpower. In order to finance these wars, the Spanish Crown had to borrow heavily from foreign bankers. With the added burden of excessive taxation, Spanish industry also fell into decline.

The events that took place during the first three decades of the Nineteenth Century brought to a conclusion the long history of the Spanish Empire. In March 1808, 100,000 French troops invaded Spain under the pretence of protecting the country's coastline from the British. Emperor Napoleon I quickly defeated the Spanish and entered Madrid in triumph.

But the Spanish people, true to their tradition of defiance towards invaders, resisted the French occupation bitterly and carried on an effective guerilla warfare. In spite of the 300,000 French troops standing on Spanish soil, their guerilla tactics never left the conquerors secure in their position. By 1813, French troops were driven from Spain, and in the following year, King Ferdinand VII was restored to his throne.

However, during the Napoleon interlude, the Spanish subjects in

SPAIN

the Americas – weary of excessive taxation and trade restrictions – made bids for political and economic autonomy that quickly developed into full-fledged wars of independence. By 1810, Mexico, Chile, Paraguay, Uruguay, Colombia, and Venezuela had all revolted, depriving Spain of its chief source of income.

Upon his restoration, King Ferdinand attempted to rebuild his authority and started to reconquer some of the colonies. But the wave of independence movements in the Western Hemisphere was gaining momentum and, by 1820, had swept the entire Spanish Americas into rebellion and civil wars that would not end until Spain had lost its last continental possession. Venezuela and Columbia gained independence in 1819, followed by Mexico in 1821.

In 1820, Spanish troops at Cádiz refused to embark for South America to risk their lives on the soil of a distant land. This mutiny spread quickly into a full-scale military revolt across all of Spain. After King Ferdinand was made a prisoner, general disorder and lawlessness spread throughout Spain. Alarmed at the civil strife and fearing its spread to other nations, the monarchies of Europe met at the Congress of Verona in 1822. At this congress, France was given permission to send its troops

SPAIN

across the Pyrenees into Spain to restore order. In 1823, 200,000 French troops entered the country and the civil strife was brought to an end.

Although King Ferdinand was returned to his throne by the French, the military power of Spain was irreparably harmed. The American revolutions continued and by 1826, Central and South America had disintegrated into eight free and independent states, shrinking Spain's once extensive and rich American empire in the New World to Cuba and Puerto Rico. Although Spain would make attempts to regain Mexico within years, her status as a maritime colonial power disappeared forever, and, in the Western Hemisphere, a multitude of new cultures would develop and evolve apart from the Spanish culture.

THE ORIGINS OF MY PEOPLE

Do the Americas have a common history? To the extent that all the Americas, from their earliest settlement to the present day, have had in occupation the people called Indians, the answer is yes. Indians are the link that binds "Latin America" to "Anglo-America." All the Americas are Indian America. Every European invader and colonizer was met by Indians, whether he came from Spain, Portugal, France, England, Sweden, or the Netherlands in the earlier days of Europe's "discovery," or whether he came from Italy or Russia or Germany in the nineteenth century. Whether he was Catholic, Protestant, Jew, Muslim, Buddhist, or Atheist, he came to the land of Indians; and no matter whether he sat down on ocean shores, river valleys, mountains, plains, or deserts, he found Indians there first....[1]

Indigenous Roots

Hispanic culture has had a profound influence on the course and direction of my family. However, the primary genetic contribution to my family has come from my Native American and indigenous ancestry. For this reason, no study of Mexico or California can be complete without an investigation into the migrations that lead the indigenous peoples to their destinations in Middle America.

---

[1] Francis Jennings, *The Founders of America* (New York: W. W. Norton & Company, 1993), p. 15.

THE ORIGINS OF MY PEOPLE

Beringia

Originally, there is said to have been a migration of people over what is now called the Bering Strait, which is located between the far eastern coast of Russian Siberia and the western coastline of Alaska. A "bridge" existed in this area because the glaciers locked up so much water that the oceans were more than three hundred feet lower 20,000 years ago than they are today. This drop in sea level exposed a massive unglaciated stretch of land, which is now referred to as the ***Bering Land Bridge.***

One thousand miles wide from north to south, this natural bridge stretched from Siberia to Alaska and was more like a subcontinent. Even at the height of the ice age, the glaciers were spotty in this area. So this subcontinent – which some archaeologists now call *Beringia* – was full of marshes and bayous and represented an ice-free corridor between glacier complexes. It was thus possible that human travelers were able to travel through this area down the east side of the Canadian Rockies towards the interior of the North American continent.[2]

---

[2] *Ibid.*, pp. 26-27.

THE ORIGINS OF MY PEOPLE

Migrations

There is a great deal of controversy about the timing of the Beringia crossings. Most archaeologists believe that the first migrants crossed Beringia sometime between 10,000 and 30,000 years ago, moving across in two or more migration waves over a long period of time, ending when the seas rose to drown the land bridge.

Dr. Scott Elias of the University of Colorado's Institute of Arctic and Alpine Research, utilizing radiocarbon dating of fossils from the youngest terrestrial sediments found on the Bering and Chukchi Sea shelves, has estimated that the link between the two continents was probably flooded around 10,500 B.P.[3] When the level of the Pacific Ocean had risen to within 100 feet of its present level, water spilled across Beringia into the Arctic Ocean and cut the Americas off from Eurasia.

These early migrations consisted of small bands of hunters who were simply following their prey across the landscape. As these Arctic travelers slowly trekked eastward, little did they realize that

---

[3] Email correspondence of Dr. Scott Elias, November 9, 2002. Dr. Elias' research employed cores that had been previously collected by the U.S. Geological Survey.

THE ORIGINS OF MY PEOPLE

many of their descendants would live in both tropical and arid climates. On the following page is a map of North America that illustrates the extent of Beringia and the possible migration routes of the early Indians.[4] It is likely that the early migrants may have traveled along the western and eastern flanks of the Rocky Mountains into what we now call the contiguous fifty states.

The primal American people adapted locally and diversely to an extraordinary variety of climatic and topographical conditions in the Americas. Traveling through and living in northern regions in which edible plants were probably scarce and of short seasonal duration, these people eventually developed the tools and weapons required of hunters, gatherers, and fishers.

In this respect, they became experts, searching out mastodons, woolly mammoths, caribou, bison, reindeer, and smaller prey. As time progressed and various groups moved south or along the coastal routes, many of these "Asians" found nourishment by catching fish, shellfish, aquatic mammals, and birds.[5]

---

[4] Illustration by Eddie Martinez.

[5] Francis Jennings, *op. cit.*, pp. 31-32.

THE ORIGINS OF MY PEOPLE

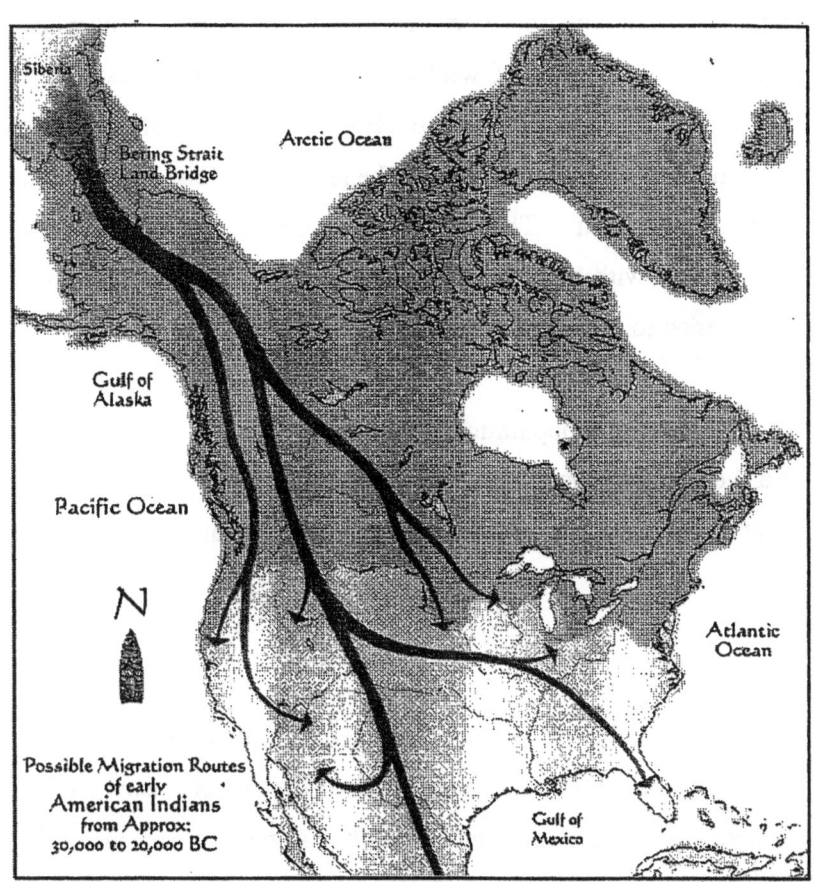

The Native American Migrations

THE ORIGINS OF MY PEOPLE

Over time, however, these first Americans would find themselves subject to what the late historian Francis Jennings had called the "iron law of population size: in proportion as human numbers increase, the adequacy of wild food resources diminishes. Land enough for ten people is not enough for twenty."[6] In short, as the population of a locality increased, the resources of the habitat were stretched to the limit. The natives came into competition with one another and with their prey, gathering the wild plants that were also needed to nourish their game.

At this point, one population group would usually split into two, and the second group would move on "over the next hill" to start what would eventually become a new cultural and linguistic group.

Cultural Diffusion

As a result of this gradual cultural diffusion, thousands of Indian societies would evolve from the original Asian stock, each having its own language, culture, and territory. A great movement of the primeval travelers took place southward along the eastern slopes of the Sierra Nevada Mountains through the Great Basin of the

---

[6] *Ibid.*, p. 41.

THE ORIGINS OF MY PEOPLE

United States, and thence through Mexico, Central America, and South America.

The author Linda Newton believes that the first travelers reached South America as early as 20,000 B.P. (Before the Present) and has estimated that they reached the tip of Tierra del Fuego in South America between 9,000 B.P. and 7,000 B.P.[7] One impressive archaeological site – Monte Verde – located in south central Chile a few miles from the Pacific Ocean, is believed to be 13,000 years old. By about 12,000 years ago, it is believed that the Indians had spread to all the unglaciated sections of both American continents.[8]

It would be impossible to determine exactly how many Indian societies came and went over the last 10,000 years. However, most anthropologists and linguists agree that when *Cristóbal Colón* (Christopher Columbus) first stepped foot in the Americas in 1492, the Native American tribes in the Western Hemisphere

---

[7] Linda Newton, "Pre-Columbian Settlement," *Cambridge Encyclopedia of Latin America and the Caribbean* (New York: Cambridge University Press, 1985), 1: pp. 128-133; Matt S. Meier and Feliciano Ribera, *Mexican Americans, American Mexicans: From Conquistadors to Chicanos* (New York: Hill and Wang, 1993), p. 10.

[8] Carlos M. Jiménez, *The Mexican American Heritage* (Berkeley: TQS Publications, 1994), pp. 26-35.

THE ORIGINS OF MY PEOPLE

may have spoken as many as 2,000 different languages and dialects.

The linguistics experts, Victor Golla and Terrence Kaufman, in their recent studies of genetic linguistics, believe that the original number of languages and language families in the Western Hemisphere at the time of contact was 1,000. Of this total, the authors believe that 325 languages families were spoken in North America, 125 in Middle America, and 550 in South America.[9]

Doctors Kaufman and Golla, however, believe that by 1950, only 600 of these languages were still surviving, with 200 in North America, 100 in Middle America, and 300 in South America. These New World languages can be further divided into eighty established language families and 83 classificatory language isolates.[10]

With these statistics in mind, we can thus envision that the original hunters and gatherers who made their way across Beringia

---

[9] Terrence Kaufman and Victor Golla, "Language Groupings in the New World: Their Reliability and Usability in Cross-Disciplinary Studies," in Colin Renfrew (ed.), *America Past, America Present: Genes and Languages in the Americas and Beyond* (Cambridge: The McDonald Institute for Archaeological Research, 2000), p. 48.

[10] *Ibid.*

THE ORIGINS OF MY PEOPLE

thousands of years ago became the ancestors of a very large and diverse group of people. Over the centuries, hundreds of ethnic groups – speaking a multitude of languages and dialects – have gradually evolved from the original stock.

THE INDIANS OF MEXICO

The ancient people who came to Mexico did not find broad connecting valleys, river systems like the Hwang Ho or the Mississippi, where people as well as streams could flow together, mingle, and become one. The "empires" which the Indians built before the coming of the Spaniards hung together loosely; the great Maya, Zapotec, Toltec-Aztec, Mixtec, and Tarascan civilizations set up hierarchies for tribute payment and created wider circles for trade, but seem barely to have spread religious beliefs and language beyond the bounds of the language group among who they originated...

When the Spaniards came they wrought a slow miracle. They began a remarkable welding together of the diverse Middle American peoples. They did this ... by the dint of hard-working and inspired missionaries, by means of the whipping post and the uprooting of thousands for forced labor...[1]

Agriculture

As the Ice Age gave way to a postglacial warming trend, the early Indians of North America learned to adapt to the climatic changes taking place. The Archaic Period, lasting from about 6,000 to 1,000 B.C., was characterized by a foraging way of life for most of the Indian tribes who survived by hunting and trapping small game, fishing, or gathering edible wild plants.[2]

---

[1] Excerpt from "Ways of Life" by Edward H. Spicer from *Six Faces of Mexico*, edited by Russell Ewing et al. (Arizona Board of Regents, 1966), p. 65. Reprinted by permission of the University of Arizona Press.

[2] Carl Waldman, *op. cit.*, p. 5.

THE INDIANS OF MEXICO

However, while many of the Indian tribes continued to live a migratory existence during this period, some innovative natives in central Mexico started to wonder how a permanent and uninterrupted supply of their most important wild plant foods could be obtained and maintained.

Somehow, the nomadic Indians in the valley of Tehuacán in south-central Mexico learned that placing the seed of *teosinte* – the grass-like ancestor of maize (corn) – in the moist soil would sprout and produce a nourishing vegetable. As soon as an Indian planted a seed in the ground, with the expectation of harvesting an edible fruit or vegetable, he became tied to the land.[3]

Archaeologists have found traces of agriculture in Mexico dating back as early as 7000 B.C. By 3400 B.C., the Mesoamerican Indians were cultivating pumpkins, beans, chili peppers, avocados, potatoes, and tobacco. With a steady and surplus food supply available, a social revolution took place in these Indian societies. Many Mexican Indian tribes started to build their first permanent dwellings, erected temples to honor their gods, and began to watch the movements of heavenly bodies. "Thus it came to be," writes

---

[3] Carlos M. Jiménez, *op. cit., p. 31.*

THE INDIANS OF MEXICO

the historian Carlos M. Jiménez, "that, in time, a flowering of the arts and sciences took place and produced the Classical Era of Indian Mexico."[4]

The Diversity of Mexico

The Republic of Mexico, consisting of 756,066 square miles,[5] has a great variety of landscapes and climates. While mountains and plateaus cover more than two-thirds of her landmass, the rest of Mexico's environment is made up of deserts, tropical forests, and fertile valleys. Mexico's many mountain ranges tend to split the country into countless smaller valleys, each forming a world of its own.

Mexico's "fragmentation into countless mountain valleys, each with its own mini-ecology," according to historian Nigel Davies, led each geographical unit to develop its own language.[6] This widespread cultural and linguistic diffusion is a key to understanding Mexican history. The remarkable diversity that resulted from this diffusion – in large part – led to Mexico's

---

[4] *Ibid.*, p. 31; Francis Jennings, *op. cit.*, pp. 40-41.

[5] Funk & Wagnalls Corporation, *The World Almanac and Book of Facts, 1995* (Mahwah, New Jersey: Funk & Wagnalls Corporation, 1994), p. 800.

[6] Nigel Davies, *The Ancient Kingdoms of Mexico* (London: Penguin Books, 1990), p. 15.

THE INDIANS OF MEXICO

conquest by the Spaniards. Speaking more than 180 mutually alien languages when the Europeans first arrived, the original Mexican Indians viewed each other with great suspicion from the earliest times.[7] When Hernán Cortés (1485-1547) came to Mexico in 1519, he found a large but fragmented collection of tribes. It was this dissension and lack of cohesion that he exploited to his advantage.

In the centuries since then, the language of each Mexican town or community has evolved independently, sometimes becoming less and less intelligible to its neighbors.[8] Thus, almost five centuries after the Conquest, the people of present-day Mexico speak more than 270 indigenous languages and dialects.[9] On the following page, our illustrator Eddie Martinez has created a map to indicate the locations of some of Mexico's most influential pre-Hispanic indigenous groups.

---

[7] J. Alden Mason, "The Native Languages of Middle America," in *The Maya and Their Neighbors* (New York: D. Appleton-Century Company, 1940), p. 58

[8] Email Communication of Pam Echerd (SIL Information), November 11, 2002.

[9] Source: "Languages of Mexico" Online: http://www.ethnologue.com/show_country.asp?name=Mexico (November 10, 2002) from Barbara F. Grimes (ed), "Ethnologue: Languages of the World" (14th edition), Dallas, Texas: SIL International, 2001.

THE INDIANS OF MEXICO

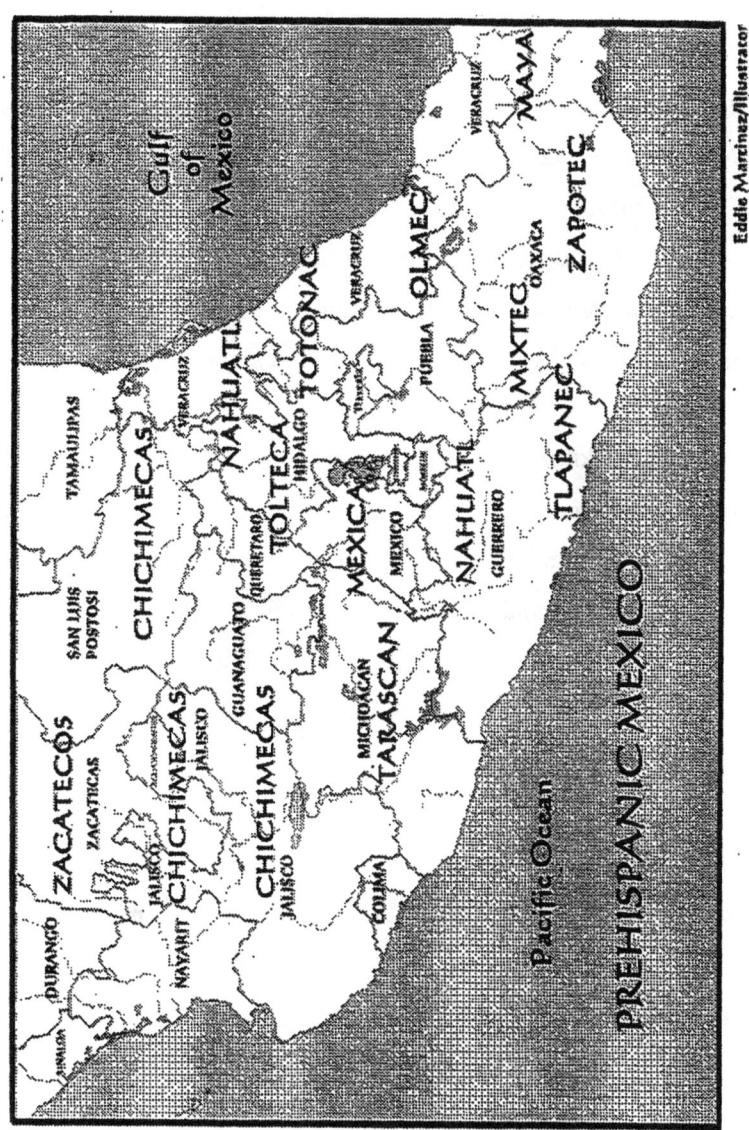

Pre-Hispanic Indigenous Groups of Mexico

THE INDIANS OF MEXICO

The Olmecs

The first monumental civilization to rise in Mexico was that of a mysterious people called the Olmecs. Living along the Gulf of Mexico coast, the Olmecs flourished in western Tabasco and southern Veracruz. Starting in 1500 B.C., they constructed earthen mounds and stone pyramids. Their civilization, which lasted a thousand years, probably peaked about 800 B.C.

Very little is known about the Olmecs, but it is believed that their decline may have been the result of multiple factors: drought, disease, and invasion from hostile neighboring tribes. However, the archaeologist and educator Richard E.W. Adams has explained that "Olmec culture did not die out, but simply was absorbed and passed on in more or less transformed variations."[10]

The Zapotecs and Mayas

Somewhat later, the Zapotec culture developed high in the Oaxaca Mountains at Monte Albán. They built magnificent temples and developed their own calendar. By A.D. 900, the Zapotec nation was in decline and Monte Albán was abandoned.

---

[10] Richard E.W. Adams, *Prehistoric Mesoamerica* (Boston: Little, Brown and Company, 1977), p. 94.

THE INDIANS OF MEXICO

The Zapotecs gradually came under the influence of the neighboring Mixtecs who, through warfare and strategic marriages, were able to establish a federation of city-states. The ancient cultures of the Zapotec and Mixtec Indians live on today among many of the Indians of the modern state of Oaxaca.

As a matter of fact, even today, no other state in the Mexican Republic exhibits the level of diversity seen within the modern state of Oaxaca. At present, sixteen different indigenous groups, speaking at least ninety languages and dialects, are recognized within the boundaries of Oaxaca. According to Mexico's National Institute of Statistics, Geography and Informatics (INEGI), 1,027,847 Oaxacan inhabitants over the age of five speak indigenous languages, representing 36.6% of the total population of the state in 1995. As a result, Oaxaca contains 18.7% of the national total of Indian language speakers in Mexico.[11]

To the south and east of the Zapotec nation, in what are now the Mexican states of Yucatán and Chiapas, the Mayan Indians developed a remarkable culture that is believed to have flourished from about A.D. 300 to A.D. 900. The Mayan Indians recorded

---

[11] Instituto Nacional de Estadística Geografía e Informática (hereinafter referred to as INEGI), "Social and Demographic Statistics," Online: http://www.inegi.gob.mx/difusion/ingles/fiest.html. November 11, 2002.

their history and built majestic cities, temples and pyramids. They also developed a practical use for the zero, an idea essential to any higher forms of mathematics. The zero would not be widely used in Europe until 1202 when the Arabs introduced it from India.[12]

The Maya devised a calendar that is considered more accurate than the one we use today. Archaeological studies have also revealed that the Maya were adept at surgery. Sometime between 600 and 700 A.D., most of the classic Mayan cities fell into decay and were abandoned by their inhabitants. The cause of the Mayan decline remains shrouded in mystery to this day.

The Valley of Mexico

The central Mexican Valley, or Anáhuac Valley, sits 8,000 feet above sea level and is surrounded by a ring of mountains and volcanoes. By definition, the Valley of Mexico is not really a valley, but an internally drained basin situated in the highlands of Mexico's central plateau.

Measuring some 60 miles from north to south, and 40 miles from east to west, the valley covered a fertile area of about 2,500 square miles in Sixteenth Century. The dominance of this central valley

---

[12] James D. Cockcroft, *Mexico: Class Formation, Capital Accumulation, and the State* (New York: Monthly Review Press, 1983), p. 12.

THE INDIANS OF MEXICO

is the hallmark of Mexico's Post-Classic Period, which lasted from about A.D. 900 until the Spanish conquest of the Sixteenth Century.[13]

An important cultural center of the central Mexican Valley was Teotihuacán (*The Place of the Gods*). As early as 200 B.C., the inhabitants of Teotihuacán began to emerge as a superior culture in the central valley. The city, situated on the eastern fringe of the Valley, was conceived in a grid pattern and laid out on a colossal scale.

The main thoroughfare, called the Avenue of the Dead, was 150 feet wide and stretched over two miles through the heart of the ceremonial center. The most striking monument in Teotihuacán is the Pyramid of the Sun. Measuring more than 700 feet at the base, the pyramid rises almost 215 feet high.[14] It is believed that the city of Teotihuacán eventually attained a population of 60,000 to 80,000 inhabitants.[15] Saburo Sugiyama of the Arizona State

---

[13] Nigel Davies, *The Aztecs: A History* (Norman, Oklahoma: University of Oklahoma Press, 1973), p. 20.

[14] Michael C. Meyer and William L. Sherman, *The Course of Mexican History* (New York: Oxford University Press, 1987), pp. 20-23.

[15] René Millon, René, "Teotihuacán: City, State and Civilization," in *Archaeology*, edited by Jeremy A. Sabloff and with the assistance of Patricia A. Andrews, *Supplement to the Handbook of Middle American Indians, vol.1*, (Austin, Texas: University of Texas Press, 1981), p. 221.

University writes that Teotihuacán was the "sixth largest city in the world during its period of greatest prosperity."[16]

Teotihuacán, for many centuries, acted as a buffer between the civilized Mexico of the south and the more primitive nomadic people who inhabited the northern regions (now represented by the modern states of Jalisco, Zacatecas, Nayarit, Durango, and Guanajuato). However, the Valley of Anáhuac, writes historian Michael C. Meyer, "was a compelling lure to rootless peoples seeking a more abundant life. With its equable climate and system of interconnecting lakes bordered by forests full of wild game, it was especially attractive to the nomads of the arid north. Because of its central location the Valley had been, from ancient times, a corridor through which tribes of diverse cultures passed – and sometimes remained."[17]

---

[16] Saburo Sugiyama, "Archaeology of Teotihuacan, Mexico," Online: http://archaeology.la.asu.edu/teo/intro/intrteo.htm. August 20, 2001. Copyright 1996, Project Temple of Quetzalcoatl, Instituto Nacional de Antropología e Historia, Mexico/ Arizona State University Department of Anthropology.

[17] Meyer and Sherman, *op. cit.*, p. 53.

THE INDIANS OF MEXICO

The Toltecs

When Teotihuacán fell in A.D. 750, the northern tribes, known by the generic term *Chichimecs* ("People of Dog Lineage"), breached the northern frontier. The most significant of these were the Tolteca-Chichimeca, or Toltecs, who were believed to have originated in southern Zacatecas.

From approximately A.D. 900 to A.D. 1100, the Toltecs became the dominant Mexican Indians in the Valley of Mexico. The Toltecs conquered and incorporated many other Indian tribes of central Mexico and extended their influence to as far south as Oaxaca. The Toltecs, however, treated their subject peoples with cruelty and arrogance, which may have played a role in their eventual demise.

The Mexica

The Mexica Indians are probably the most well known of all Mexico's ancient cultures. This indigenous group had very obscure and humble roots that made their rise to power during the Fifteenth and Sixteenth Centuries even more remarkable.

The Mexica (pronounced "me-shee-ka") Indians represent the most dominant ethnic group within the larger cultural group that we refer to as the Aztecs. All of the Aztec peoples spoke the

THE INDIANS OF MEXICO

Náhuatl language, which – in 2000 – was still spoken by 1,448,936 Mexicans. As such the total population of Náhuatl speakers in the present day represents 24 percent of the total indigenous-speaking population of Mexico (6,044,547).[18]

Legend tells us that in A.D. 1111, the Mexica Indians left their home in *Aztlán* (The Place of Herons), believed to be located in northwestern Mexico. It is important to note, however, that the Aztlan migrations were not one simple movement of a single group of people.

Instead, as the anthropologist Professor Michael E. Smith of the University of New York, has noted, "when all of the native histories are compared, no fewer than seventeen ethnic groups are listed among the original tribes migrating from Aztlán..." Professor Smith also writes that "the north to south movement of the Aztlan groups is supported by research in historical linguistics."[19]

---

[18] INEGI, *Estados Unidos Mexicanos. XII Censo General de Población y Vivienda, 2000. Tabulados Básicos y por Entidad Federativa. Bases de Datos y Tabulados de la Muestra Censal.*

[19] Michael E. Smith, *The Aztecs* (Cambridge, Massachusetts: Blackwell Publishers, Inc., 1996), pp. 39, 41.

THE INDIANS OF MEXICO

"The Náhuatl language," explains Professor Smith, is "classified in the Nahuan group of the Uto-Aztecan family of languages." As such, the language of the Aztecs is "unrelated to most Mesoamerican language families" and "was a relatively recent intrusion into Mesoamerica."[20] It is believed that the migrations southward probably took place over several generations. "Led by priests," continues Professor Smith, "the migrants... stopped periodically to build houses and temples, to gather and cultivate food, and to carry out rituals."[21]

After wandering for many years, the various groups eventually arrived in the Valley of Mexico and in neighboring areas. The Mexica were the last to arrive, perhaps around A.D. 1250. Because all of the good land was already occupied, the Mexica were forced to settle in what Professor Smith calls "an undesirable, desolate area of the Valley of Mexico called Chapultepec, 'grasshopper hill' or 'place of the grasshopper.'"[22]

In A.D. 1327, the Aztecs established a new home for themselves in the middle of Lake Texcoco, where they founded their capital

---

[20] *Ibid.*, p. 41.

[21] *Ibid.*, p. 39.

[22] *Ibid.*, p. 40.

THE INDIANS OF MEXICO

city of Tenochtitlán. Fifteen years after the founding of Tenochtitlán, the Aztecs achieved dominance in the Valley by forming a triple alliance with their neighbors at Texcoco and Tlacopan.

The Aztec Empire

By the end of the Fifteenth Century, the Mexica had established an elaborate and wide-ranging empire that extended to the Mexican states of Guerrero and Colima. This empire consisted of a diverse population that is believed to have numbered between 10 and 25 million people. The population of Tenochtitlán is believed to have reached 300,000, making it larger than Madrid or Rome.[23] Probably only four cities in Europe – Paris, Venice, Milan, and Naples – had a greater population at this time.

With each conquest, the Aztec domain had become more and more ethnically diverse, eventually controlling thirty-eight provinces. But the most important component of this massive empire was the tribute that the Mexica demanded from the various city-states and subject chieftains. This tribute took many forms, including

---

[23] Henry F. Dobyns, "Estimating Aboriginal American Population, *Current Anthropology* 7 (1966), pp. 395-449; James D. Cockcroft, *op. cit.*, pp. 7, 320.

THE INDIANS OF MEXICO

textiles, warriors' costumes, foodstuffs, maize, beans, chilies, cacao, bee honey, salt and human beings (for sacrificial rituals).

The constant demand for tribute goods transformed the Aztec Empire. "When one considers that imperial tribute pouring into the capital two to four times a year together with trade goods imported by Aztec merchants, the volume of incoming wealth was immense."[24] However, this policy – so greedy and hateful to the subject peoples – laid the foundation for the eventual destruction of Tenochtitlán.

In May 1521, Hernán Cortés, with a force of 900 Spaniards and a hundred thousand allied Indian warriors laid siege to Tenochtitlán. The Aztec defenders resisted to the last until their people were reduced to eating worms and bark from trees.

On August 13, 1521, after a 75-day siege, Tenochtitlán finally fell. In later years, Aztec historians would state that 240,000 Aztecs died in the siege. And the great empire which had been assembled over the previous century disintegrated. The Spanish conquest of Mexico had begun.

---

[24] Michael E. Smith, *op. cit.*, p. 185.

INDIGENOUS MEXICAN ROOTS

Two of the major tribes who maintained their identities throughout the conquest and into the Twentieth Century were the Cahitan-speaking Mayos and Yaquis. They were of nearly identical language and cultural background, but their reactions to the Spaniards who first encountered them were very different. The Mayos consistently sought friendly alliance with the Spaniards for the first two hundred years of contact. The Yaquis, on the other hand, resisted armed intrusion in their territory from the first, and were so successful that they were able to set their own terms for the entrance of missionaries.[1]

It quickly became apparent to the northward-pushing Conquistadores that they had here entered a different cultural world from the Aztec-dominated one which they had first encountered in Mexico.[2]

La Madre Patria: Sinaloa y Sonora

California is my ancestral homeland. It is the only home that recent generations of my family have known and it is a matter of pride for all of my family. However, my identity as a Mexican American is also strong. Although my mother's family has lived in California since the Eighteenth Century, there has been an ongoing infusion of the Mexican culture over the last century and a half.

---

[1] Excerpt from *Edward H. Spicer: Cycles of Conquest* by Edward H. Spicer (Tucson: Arizona Board of Regents, 1962), p. 46. Reprinted by permission of the University of Arizona Press.

[2] *Ibid.*, p. 8. Reprinted by permission of the University of Arizona Press.

INDIGENOUS MEXICAN ROOTS

Many of my California ancestors married male immigrants who came from the interior of Mexico to California. Even my maternal grandmother, Dora, married a *Bracero* laborer (Eusebio Basulto) who left Jalisco for the United States during World War II. This fact alone means that one-quarter of my ancestors are from that west central state of Mexico.

Because of this continuous contribution, our Mexican-American identity has remained strong and intact. But, it is important to note that almost all of my earliest California ancestors also came from Mexico, specifically Sinaloa and Sonora. Thus, it is possible for me to say that the Mexican states of Sinaloa and Sonora are as much my ancestral homeland as are Los Angeles and Santa Barbara. Nearly all of los pobladores and los soldados de cuera in the Expedition of 1781 came from those two states and – well into the Nineteenth Century – many Californians referred to both Sonora and Sinaloa as la madre patria (Motherland).[3]

My entire family speaks both English and Spanish. The Spanish language was inherited from my grandparents, my great-grandparents, and all of my ancestors before them. But our indigenous ancestry is also an important part of our cultural

---

[3] Rios-Bustamante and Pedro Castillo, *op. cit.*, p. 24.

INDIGENOUS MEXICAN ROOTS

heritage. We speak no Indian languages, but we are well aware of our descent from the indigenous peoples who inhabited our ancestral homelands in Sinaloa and Sonora.

For this reason, we look to the Amerindian populations of Sinaloa and Sonora as our forebears. Like the rest of Mexico, the northwestern region of Mexico boasted a great diversity of indigenous cultures when the Spaniards first arrived in the area in 1531. To give the reader a clear idea of this wonderful diversity, our illustrator, Eddie Martinez, has produced a map – shown on the following page – indicating the linguistic divisions of northwestern Mexico and portions of the Great Southwest. In the pages that follow, we will discuss the events that transpired after the Spaniards first arrived in the area.

First Contact (1531)

In December 1529, the professional lawyer turned Conquistador, Nuño Beltrán de Guzmán, led an expedition of 300 Spaniards and 10,000 Indian allies (Tlaxcalans, Aztecs and Tarascans) into the coastal region of what is now called Sinaloa.

INDIGENOUS MEXICAN ROOTS

The Indigenous People of Northwestern Mexico

INDIGENOUS MEXICAN ROOTS

Before arriving in the coastal region, Guzmán's army had ravaged through Michoacán, Jalisco, Zacatecas, and Nayarit, provoking the natives to give battle everywhere he went. The historian Peter Gerhard, in *The North Frontier of New Spain*, observed that "Guzmán's strategy throughout was to terrorize the natives with often unprovoked killing, torture, and enslavement... The army left a path of corpses and destroyed houses and crops, impressing surviving males into service and leaving women and children to starve."[4]

In March 1531, Guzmán's army reached the site of present-day Culiacán (now in Sinaloa), where his force engaged an army of 30,000 warriors in a pitched battle. The indigenous forces were decisively defeated.

The indigenous people confronted by Guzmán belonged to the Cáhita language group. Speaking eighteen closely related dialects, the Cáhita peoples of Sinaloa and Sonora numbered about 115,000 and were the most numerous of any single language group in northern Mexico. These Indians inhabited the coastal area of northwestern Mexico along the lower courses of the Sinaloa, Fuerte, Mayo, and Yaqui Rivers.

---

[4] Peter Gerhard, *The Northern Frontier of New Spain* (Princeton, New Jersey: Princeton University Press, 1982), pp. 42-43.

INDIGENOUS MEXICAN ROOTS

During his stay in Sinaloa, Guzmán's army was ravaged by an epidemic that killed many of his Amerindian auxiliaries. Finally, in October 1531, after establishing San Miguel de Culiacán on the San Lorenzo River, Guzmán returned to the south, his mostly indigenous army decimated by hunger and disease. But the Spanish post at Culiacán remained, Mr. Gerhard writes, as "a small outpost of Spaniards... surrounded on all sides but the sea by hostile Indians kept in a state of agitation" by the slave-hunting activities of the Spaniards.[5] Nuño de Guzmán was eventually brought to justice for his genocidal actions.

Epidemic Disease

Daniel T. Reff, the author of *Disease, Depopulation, and Culture Change in Northwestern New Spain, 1518-1764*, explains that "viruses and other microorganisms undergo significant genetic changes when exposed to a new host environment, changes often resulting in new and more virulent strains of microorganisms." The Indians of the coastal region, never having been exposed to the Spaniards and their diseases previously, provided fertile ground for the proliferation of smallpox and measles. It is believed that as many as 130,000 people died in the Valley of Culiacán

---

[5] *Ibid.*, p. 258.

INDIGENOUS MEXICAN ROOTS

during the Measles Pandemic of 1530-1534 and the Smallpox Plague of 1535-1536.[6]

As the Spaniards moved northward they found an amazing diversity of indigenous groups. Unlike the more concentrated Amerindian groups of central Mexico, the Indians of the north were referred to as "ranchería people" by the Spaniards. Their fixed points of settlements (rancherías) were usually scattered over an area of several miles and one dwelling may be separated from the next by up to half a mile. The renowned anthropologist, Professor Edward H. Spicer (1906-1983), writing in *Cycles of Conquest: The Impact of Spain, Mexico, and the United States on the Indians of the Southwest, 1533-1960*, observed that most ranchería people were agriculturalists and farming was their primary activity.[7]

Distant Enclave

In 1533, Diego de Guzmán (the nephew of Nuño) fought a brief battle with the Yaquis along the banks of the Yaqui River. "His force dispersed the Indians," notes Professor Spicer, "... but he

---

[6] Daniel T. Reff, *Disease, Depopulation, and Culture Change in Northwestern New Spain, 1518-1764* (Salt Lake City: University of Utah Press, 1991), pp. 100-114.

[7] Edward H. Spicer, *op. cit.*, pp. 12-13.

nevertheless seems to have lost heart for further conquest and did not follow up his victory. He was greatly impressed with the fighting ability of the Yaquis who opposed him."[8]

Thus, the small province of Culiacán, according to Peter Gerhard, "became a distant enclave of Spanish power, separated by a hundred miles of hostile territory from the rest of" the Spanish Empire.[9] In 1562, the area was included in the newly established Spanish province of Nueva Vizcaya (which – at the time – included the modern day states of Sonora, Sinaloa, Chihuahua and Durango).

In 1599, Captain Diego de Hurdaide established San Felipe y Santiago on the site of the modern city of Sinaloa. From here, Captain Hurdaide waged a vigorous military campaign that subjugated the Cáhita-speaking Indians of the Fuerte River – the Sinaloas, Tehuecos, Zuaques, and Ahomes. Initially, these indigenous groups, numbering approximately 20,000 people, resisted strongly, but eventually they were subdued.

---

[8] *Ibid.*, p. 46.

[9] Peter Gerhard, *op. cit.*, p. 45.

INDIGENOUS MEXICAN ROOTS

The Mayo and Yaqui Indians

The Mayo Indians were an important Cáhita-speaking tribe occupying some fifteen towns along the Mayo and Fuerte rivers of southern Sonora and northern Sinaloa. As early as 1601, they had developed a curious interest in the Jesuit-run missions of their neighbors.

The Mayos sent delegations to inspect the Catholic churches and, as Professor Spicer observes, "were so favorably impressed that large groups of Mayos numbering a hundred or more also made visits and became acquainted with Jesuit activities." As the Jesuits began their spiritual conquest of the Mayos, Captain Hurdaide, in 1609, signed a peace treaty with the military leaders of the Mayos.[10]

At contact, the Yaqui Indians occupied the coastal region of Sonora along the Yaqui River. Divided into eighty autonomous communities, their primary activity was agriculture. Although the Yaqui Indians had resisted Spanish advances in 1531 and 1533, they had welcomed Spanish explorers who came in peace in 1565, apparently in the hopes of winning the Spaniards as allies in their wars against their Mayo neighbors.

---

[10] Edward H. Spicer, *op. cit.*, pp. 46-47.

INDIGENOUS MEXICAN ROOTS

In 1609, as Captain Hurdaide became engaged with the pacification of the Ocoronis (another Cahita-speaking group of northern Sinaloa), he reached the Yaqui River, where he was confronted by a group of Yaquis. Then, in 1610, with the Mayo Indians as his primary allies, Captain Hurdaide returned to Yaqui territory with a force of 2,000 Indians and forty Spanish soldiers. He was soundly defeated. When he returned with another force of 4,000 Indian foot soldiers and fifty mounted Spanish cavalry, he was again defeated in a bloody daylong battle.[11]

In 1613, at their own request, the Mayos accepted Jesuit missionaries. Soon after, the first mission was established in Mayo territory by the Jesuit Father Pedro Mendez. In the first fifteen days, more than 3,000 persons received baptism. By 1620, with 30,000 persons baptized, the Mayos had been concentrated in seven mission towns.

In 1617, the Yaquis, utilizing the services of Mayo intermediaries, invited the Jesuit missionaries to begin their work among them. Professor Spicer noted that after observing the Mayo-Jesuit interactions that started in 1613, the Yaquis seemed to be impressed with the Jesuits. Bringing a message of everlasting life,

---

[11] *Ibid.*, p. 47.

the Jesuits impressed the Yaquis with their good intentions and their spirituality. Their concern for the well being of the Indians won the confidence of the Yaqui people. In seeking to protect the Yaqui from exploitation by mine owners and encomenderos, the Jesuits came into direct conflict with the Spanish political authorities. From 1617 to 1619, nearly 30,000 Yaquis were baptized. By 1623, the Jesuits had reorganized the Yaquis from about eighty rancherías into eight mission villages.[12]

For more than a century, the Yaqui and Mayo Indians lived in peaceful coexistence with the Spanish administrators and padres. Spaniards. In 1733, both Sinaloa and Sonora were detached from Nueva Vizcaya and given recognition as the province of Sonora y Sinaloa. However, by this time rifts in the relationship of the Spaniards with their indigenous subjects started to appear.

As silver mining increased in the town of Álamos, more and more Spanish settlers had entered the area. "With the coming of the settlers," writes Dr. Spicer, "encroachment on Indian lands took

---

[12] *Ibid.*, pp. 48-49; Susan M. Deeds, "Indigenous Rebellions on the Northern Mexican Mission Frontier: From First-Generation to Later Colonial Responses," in Donna J. Guy and Thomas E. Sheridan (eds.), *Contested Ground: Comparative Frontiers on the Northern and Southern Edges of the Spanish Empire* (Tucson: University of Arizona Press, 1998), pp. 40-41

INDIGENOUS MEXICAN ROOTS

place, and the frictions between the Indians and Spaniards began."[13]

Dr. Susan M. Deeds of the Northern Arizona University has studied the indigenous rebellions in Sinaloa and Sonora. In describing the causes of this rebellion, Dr. Deeds observes that the Jesuits had ignored "growing Yaqui resentment over lack of control of productive resources." During the last half of the Seventeenth Century, so much agricultural surplus was produced that storehouses were built to store the food and send it to other missions in the frontier zone. This situation was complicated by a poor harvest in 1739, followed in 1740 by severe flooding which exacerbated food shortages.[14]

Dr. Deeds also points out that the "increasingly bureaucratic and inflexible Jesuit organization... obdurately disregarded Yaqui demands for autonomy in the selection of their own village officials" Thus, this rebellion, writes Ms. Deeds, was "a more limited endeavor to restore the colonial pact of village autonomy and territorial integrity."[15] At the beginning of the revolt, an

---

[13] Edward H. Spicer, *op. cit.*, p. 51.

[14] Susan M. Deeds, *op. cit.*, pp. 41-43.

[15] *Ibid.*, pp. 42-43.

articulate leader named El Muni emerged in the Yaqui community. El Muni and another Yaqui leader, Bernabé, took the Yaquis' grievances to local civil authorities. Resenting this undermining of their authority, the Jesuits had Muni and Bernabé arrested.

The arrests triggered a spontaneous outcry, with two thousand armed indigenous men gathering to demand the release of the two leaders. The Governor, having heard the complaints of both sides, recommended that the Yaqui leaders go to Mexico City to testify personally before the Viceroy and Archbishop Vizrón. In February 1740, the Archbishop approved all of the Yaqui demands for free elections, respect for land boundaries, that Yaquis be paid for work, and that they not be forced to work in mines.

The initial stages of the 1740 revolt saw sporadic and uncoordinated activity in Sinaloa and Sonora, primarily taking place in the Mayo territory (in the south) or in the Lower Pima Country (to the north). Catholic churches were burned to the ground while priests and settlers were driven out, fleeing to the silver mining town at Alamos. Eventually, Juan Calixto raised an army of 6,000 composed of Pima, Yaqui and Mayo Indians. With this large force, Calixto gained control of all the towns along the Mayo and Yaqui Rivers.[16]

However, in August 1740, Captain Agustín de Vildósola defeated the insurgents. The rebellion cost the lives of a thousand Spaniards and more than 5,000 Indians. After the 1740 rebellion, the new Governor of Sonora began a program of secularization by posting garrisons in the Yaqui Valley and encouraging Spanish residents to return to the area of rebellion.

The Apache Threat

The word "Apache" comes from the Yuma word for "fighting-men". It also comes from a Zuni word meaning "enemy". Professor Cynthia Radding, the author of "The Colonial Pact and Changing Ethnic Frontiers in Highland Sonora, 1740-1840," refers to the Apaches as "diverse bands" of hunter-gatherers "related linguistically to the Athapaskan speakers of Alaska and western Canada."[17]

---

[16] *Ibid.*, pp. 42-43; Edward H. Spicer, *op. cit.*, pp. 51-53.
[17] Cynthia Radding, "The Colonial Pact and Changing Ethnic Frontiers in Highland Sonora, 1740-1840" in in Donna J. Guy and Thomas E. Sheridan (eds.), *Contested Ground: Comparative Frontiers on the Northern and Southern Edges of the Spanish Empire* (Tucson: University of Arizona Press, 1998), p. 55.

INDIGENOUS MEXICAN ROOTS

The Apaches were composed of six regional groups: (1) the Western Apaches (Coyotero) of eastern Arizona; (2) the Chiricahua of southwestern New Mexico, southeastern Arizona, Chihuahua and Sonora; (3) the Mescalero of southern New Mexico; (4) the Jicarilla of Colorado, northern New Mexico and northwestern Texas; (5) the Lipan Apache of New Mexico and Texas; and (6) the Kiowa Apache of Colorado, Oklahoma, and Texas.

The first Apache raids on Sonora appear to have taken place during the early part of the late Seventeenth Century. In fact, to counter the early Apache thrusts into Sonora, presidios were established at Janos (1685) in Chihuahua and at Fronteras (1690) in northern Opata country. The Apache depredations continued into the Eighteenth Century and prompted Captain Juan Mateo Mange in 1737 to report that "many mines have been destroyed, 15 large estancias along the frontier has been totally destroyed, having lost two hundred head of cattle, mules, and horses; several missions have been burned and two hundred Christians have lost their lives to the Apache enemy, who sustains himself only with the bow and arrow, killing and stealing livestock. All this has left us in ruins."

INDIGENOUS MEXICAN ROOTS

In the 1750s, the fiercest of all Apache tribes, the Chiricahua, began hunting and raiding along the mountainous frontier regions of both Sonora and Chihuahua. The pressure of constant warfare waged against these nomads led the Spanish military to adopt a policy of maintaining armed garrisons of paid soldiers (presidios) in the problem areas.

By 1760, Spain boasted a total of twenty-three presidios in the frontier regions. But the Apaches were highly skilled horsemen who were able to elude presidio troops and to continue striking terror into the small frontier settlements. Professor Robert Salmon, the author of *Indian Revolts in Northern New Spain: A Synthesis of Resistance (1680-1786)* writes that the continuing Indian attacks eventually "broke the chain of ineffective presidios established to control them" and, as the end of the Eighteenth Century approached, became a major threat to the continued Spanish occupation of Sonora and Chihuahua. And, as Mr. Salmon concludes, "Indian warriors exacted high tolls in commerce, livestock, and lives."[18]

---

[18] Robert Mario Salmon, *Indian Revolts in Northern New Spain: A Synthesis of Resistance (1680-1786)* (Lanham, Maryland: University Press of America, Inc., 1991)., p. 1.

INDIGENOUS MEXICAN ROOTS

As my Sinaloa and Sonora ancestors prepared to make their way through hostile territory to California in the Expedition of 1781, the Apache threat weighed heavily on their minds.

SINALOA AND SONORA

Beyond the Yaqui River was Sonora. Spanish occupation of this remote region did not begin until the early seventeenth century. First to come were missionaries, soldiers, and miners. Civil settlements soon followed.... The continued threat of Indian depredations and periodical serious uprisings among the Seri, Yaqui, and Pima Indians plagued the advance of the frontier beyond Sinaloa. In the latter half of the Eighteenth Century Apache raids created a major threat to the continued occupation of Spanish communities in Sonora... Apache bands raided frequently deep into Nueva Vizcaya and Sonora, taking foodstuffs, livestock, and slaves from among the Christianized Indians and the scattered, ill-defended Spanish communities. As a result, Sonora never developed beyond frontier status during the Spanish era, unlike its neighbor Sinaloa.[1]

Sonora

The Mexican state of Sonora in northwestern Mexico is bounded on the north by the United States, on the east by Chihuahua, on the south by Sinaloa, and on the west by the Gulf of California and a small portion of Baja California. Sonora, with an area of 71,625 square miles, is actually Mexico's second largest state and is a very mountainous area, except for the coastal plains that lay along the Gulf of California.

As we have seen, the Spaniards were unable to subdue the indigenous peoples of Sonora until the Seventeenth Century. But,

---

[1] Excerpt from Oakah L. Jones, Jr., *Los Paisanos: Spanish Settlers on the Northern Frontier of New Spain* (Norman: University of Oklahoma Press, 1978), p. 177. Reprinted by permission of the University of Oklahoma Press.

SINALOA AND SONORA

as the mineral wealth of this region became more obvious, the colonial authorities took important steps to secure the vast copper, gold, lead and silver deposits in the area. In lesser amounts, Spanish entrepreneurs would also find zinc, coal, and gypsum.

Álamos

Several branches of my family – the Valenzuela, Parra, Feliz, and Quintero families – came from the mining city of Álamos, which is located in the Sierra Madre foothills of Sonora, about forty miles east of the Gulf of California and 135 miles southeast of Guaymas. On the following page, we have reproduced a map showing the political districts of Sinaloa and Sonora in 1786.[2] Other branches of my pioneer family came from Fuerte (the Fernandez family) and Rosario (the Olivas family), both of which are located in present-day state of Sinaloa.

In 1531, the Spanish conquistador, Francisco Coronado, first passed through this area on his way north. The pueblo of Álamos, named for the cottonwood trees found in that area, was founded in 1540 as a camp for one of Francisco Coronado's expeditions. Not until 1630 did the Jesuits found their first mission in this town.

---

[2] Peter Gerhard, *op. cit.*, p. 247. Reprinted by permission of Princeton University Press.

SINALOA AND SONORA

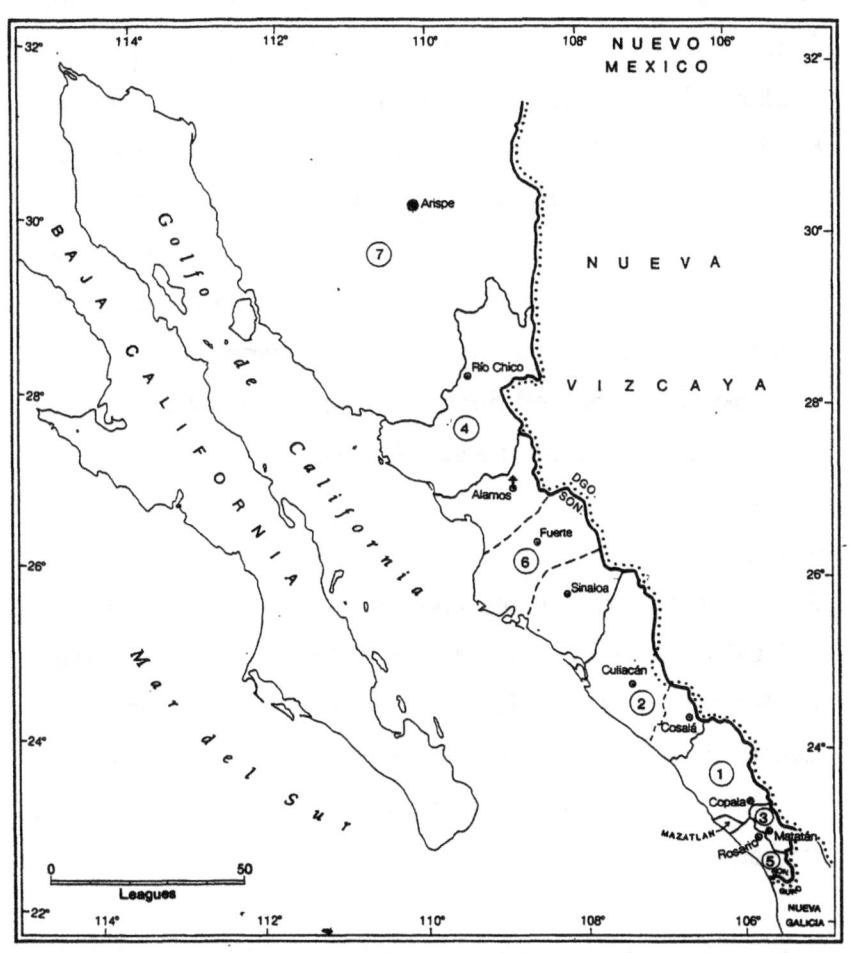

Sinaloa and Sonora in 1786

SINALOA AND SONORA

In 1683, one of Mexico's richest silver strikes – the Europa Mine – was made near the Rio de Mayo not far from Álamos. The result of this strike, writes Peter Gerhard, is that Álamos "became the largest settlement in the northwest, with the mixed-race floating population common to such mining centers."[3] In the last half of the Eighteenth Century, the population of Álamos reached 30,000 and the town itself earned the title, "Silver Capital of the World." In 1781, Álamos would be the departure point for the great expedition that left Sonora to establish the pueblo of Los Angeles and the presidio of Santa Barbara.

Sinaloa

Sinaloa is bordered on the north by the states of Sonora and Chihuahua, on the south by Nayarit and on the east by Durango. On Sinaloa's west lay 410 miles of coastline facing the Pacific Ocean. As Mexico's seventeenth largest state, Sinaloa has an area of 58,092 square miles, encompassing 2.9% of Mexico's total territory.

Sinaloa is a long narrow state extending along the Gulf of California and the Pacific Ocean. Its narrow coastal lowlands are cut by many streams that flow westward from the Sierra Madre

---

[3] *Ibid.*, p. 277; Roger Dunbier, *The Sonoran Desert – Its Geography, Economy, and People* (Tucson: University of Arizona Press, 1968), pp. 151-152.

SINALOA AND SONORA

Occidental. Today, Sinaloa is an important agricultural state. It is an important producer of tomatoes, cucumbers, pumpkins, chilies, eggplants, mangoes, cantaloupes, watermelons, soybeans, wheat and sorghum.

Rosario

Located in the southernmost corner of Sinaloa, the colonial silver-mining city of Rosario is 38 miles southeast of Mazatlán and almost 200 miles south of Culiacán (the capital of Sinaloa). Rosario's Baroque-style church, Nuestra Señora de Rosario – which my Olivas ancestors attended – is principal tourist attraction.

Rosario sits along the Baluarte River on the coastal floodplain astride the mountain ranges that lay a short distance inland. "At contact," according to Peter Gerhard, "the floodplain supported a large population of farmers and fishermen speaking Totorame, a Cora (Nahuatoid) dialect." A settlement called Chametlan (Caulian in the Totorame dialect) stood on the low terraces along both sides of the Baluarte River.[4]

---

[4] Peter Gerhard, *op. cit.*, p. 270.

SINALOA AND SONORA

Like her neighbor Sonora, Sinaloa became famous for its abundant mineral resources, which included deposits of silver, gold, and copper. In 1655, a prospector discovered a rich vein of silver and gold, leading to the establishment of the mining center of Nuestra Señora del Rosario.[5] It has been said that more than seventy kilometers of underground arteries were dug through the Rosario mines in a time span of 290 years.

Rosario was described in 1686 as "a fine little town of about 60 or 70 houses... chiefly inhabited with Indians," and an Eighteenth Century report describes the settlement as a predominantly mestizo-mulato settlement and an important trading center. The population reached 5,618 by the 1790.[6] Today, the region surrounding Rosario is a major producer of cotton, sugar cane, fruits, and vegetables.

El Fuerte

The colonial town of El Fuerte is located in the northern part of Sinaloa, about 110 miles from Álamos. In 1564, this settlement – which was the ancestral town for my Fernandez ancestors – was

---

[5] *Ibid.*, p. 272.

[6] *Ibid.*, p. 272; Archivo General de la Nación, (Distrito Federal, Mexico), 522, fol. 272.

SINALOA AND SONORA

founded by Francisco de Ibarra with the name San Juan Bautista de Carapoa. However, as Mr. Gerhard has noted, the Spanish "force was too small to control the still populous Indian communities, and they were obliged to retreat to Culiacán in 1569-1570." The Spaniards returned in 1583 and "the tiny settlement persevered in the face of Indian hostility until reinforcements, along with Jesuit missionaries, arrived in 1589-1591."[7]

Indian rebellions took place in this area in 1594, 1599, 1604, and 1611-1613. Faced with hostile neighbors (the Zuaque and Tehueco Indians), the Spaniards constructed a fort in 1610 to protect the small settlement. This fort remains a tourist attraction today.

By the last half of the Eighteenth Century, El Fuerte had obtained some level of security with a population of at least 5,000 people. Today, the region surrounding Rosario is a significant producer of agricultural crops.

One Step Up the Social Ladder
One might be inclined to ask the question, "Why did your ancestors leave a dangerous frontier zone (Sonora) for a land that

---

[7] Peter Gerhard, *op. cit.*, p. 274.

was barely explored and inhabited by large numbers of potentially-hostile indigenous forces?"

The author and historian, Dr. Antonio Ríos-Bustamante, has studied the factors that motivated the soldiers from Sinaloa and Sonora to volunteer for such a dangerous assignment. Significantly, he explains, "the original settlers of Los Angeles were racially mixed persons of Indian, African, and European descent. This mixed racial composition was typical of both the settlers of Alta California and of the majority of the population of the northwest coast provinces of Mexico from which they were recruited."[8]

In the century preceding the Expedition of 1781, many Indians in Sonora and Sinaloa had been "culturally assimilated and ethnically intermixed into the Spanish-speaking mestizo society."[9] From the available church and census records, it appears that most of my ancestors fell into this category.

---

[8] Antonio Rios-Bustamante, *Mexican Los Angeles* (Encino, California: Floricano Press, 1992), pp. 35-36.

[9] Antonio Rios-Bustamante and Pedro Castillo, *An Illustrated History of Mexican Los Angeles, 1781-1985* (Los Angeles: University of California, 1986), p. 24.

SINALOA AND SONORA

Dr. Rios-Bustamante writes that Sonora and Sinaloa "had developed certain social and economic stratification. Both regions reflected this division in the widening gap between the small group of provincial elite (wealthy mineowners, land-owners, merchants, and officials) and the already burgeoning lower classes. In Sinaloa, especially, the chances for economic and social advancement were limited." And "in fact, the ownership of even a small farm was beyond the reach of the working classes."[10]

In stark contrast, the frontera (frontier) offered great possibilities to those willing to risk the hardships and labors of the journey. Dr. Rios-Bustamante continued, "To those willing to work hard, a military posting in Alta California, "promised high wages and the chance to own or, at least, to use land. For many young men, enlistment in a company of presidial soldiers meant a regular salary and, perhaps, a future promotion to corporal or sergeant. Moreover, it meant the possibility of a small land grant upon retirement. Of course, the risks were correspondingly great, as was the reluctance of people to leave their birthplaces."[11]

---

[10] *Ibid.*, p. 25.

[11] Ibid.

ALTA CALIFORNIA

> *One of the great ironies of history is that California was the last imperial colony established by Spain. It was founded during the budding American revolt against British colonial rule, 1768-81. What provoked Spain to undertake this last colonial venture? Pure and simple, the founding of California was motivated solely by the policy of defensive expansion.*[1]

Early Expeditions

After the conquest of Tenochtitlán (Mexico City) in 1521, Hernán Cortés immediately began to look for new horizons to conquer. With the former capital of the Mexica as his base, Cortés sent expeditions to explore the vast spaces to the north and west. By 1522, Spanish forces had already reached the Pacific coast in the present-day province of Michoacán, where Cortés founded a settlement at Zacatula.[2]

On June 27, 1542, Captain Juan Rodriguez Cabrillo, a Portuguese navigator sailing under the flag of Spain, left the Port of Navidad in present-day Jalisco. His goal was to locate the fabled strait of Anian, a reputed northwest passage that connected the Atlantic Ocean with the Pacific Ocean. On September 28, 1542, Cabrillo's ships reached what we now call San Diego Bay. Sailing northward

---

[1] Doyce B. Nunis, Jr. (ed), *Southern California's Spanish Heritage: An Anthology* (Los Angeles: Historical Society of Southern California, 1992), p. xxi.

[2] Charles E. Chapman, *op. cit.*, p. 44.

ALTA CALIFORNIA

along the coastline, Cabrillo entered the Santa Barbara Channel on October 13, 1542, claiming both the Channel Islands and the mainland for the King of Spain. However, not for another 227 years would a Spaniard set his feet upon the mainland with the intention of staying.

Foreign Threats

During most of the Sixteenth Century, Spain's domination of the high seas was virtually unchallenged. But, starting with the defeat of the Spanish Armada in 1588, the English, Dutch, and French fleets began a sustained effort to supplant the Spaniards as masters of the "Seven Seas." By the 1770s, the English colonies along the Atlantic coast of North America had increased in both size and power. In addition, English and French fur traders were now pushing into the western watersheds of the Mississippi River.

But most importantly, the Russians were now exploring resources along the northwestern coast of North America in the area of present-day Oregon with their eyes pointed toward the coastline of Alta California.

Then, in 1768, the Spanish ambassador to Russia reported that the Russians were planning to occupy the area around California's

ALTA CALIFORNIA

Monterey Bay. The potential value of Monterey's harbor had already been discovered several years earlier, and the news of this proposed Russian move sounded alarms in Madrid. In order to counter this serious challenge to Spain's claims on the California coastline, King Carlos III in 1774 issued an edict calling for the fortification and settlement of Alta California.

Nine years earlier, the King had already appointed a royal bureaucrat named General José de Gálvez as the Visitor-General of New Spain. A man of great intelligence and energy, Gálvez immediately formulated a vigorous expansion program that would consolidate Spanish power in all of the northern provinces of Nueva España. As a crucial part of Gálvez' plan, Governor Gáspar de Portola and Father Junipero Serra (1713-1784) were commissioned to expand the northwest frontier of *Nueva España* in order to make *Alta California* a buffer zone against the foreign intrusion of the Russians and British. In pursuit of this task, four land and sea expeditions were sent into Alta California between January and May 1769.[3]

---

[3] Antonio Rios-Bustamante and Pedro Castillo, *op. cit.*, p.20.

ALTA CALIFORNIA

The primary objective of the expeditions was to send soldiers under the command of Gáspar de Portolá to occupy the port at Monterey Bay and establish a *presidio* (military garrison) there. The second objective, under the guidance and direction of Father Junipero Serra, was to establish missions at both Monterey and San Diego. Father Junipero Serra was no stranger to the business of managing missions. In 1767, he had been appointed the President of the fourteen missions in Baja California that had been founded by the Jesuits before their abrupt expulsion by King Carlos III in the same year.[4]

---

[4] Iris H. W. Engstrand, *Serra's San Diego: Father Junipero Serra and California's Beginnings* (San Diego, California: 1982), p. 6.

SPANISH COLONIAL INSTITUTIONS

The Presidio was but one of three separate yet related colonial institutions employed by Imperial Spain in its drive northward from Central Mexico into what is now the American Southwest. The other two were the mission and civil settlement. On paper these institutions seemed excellent devices for conquering, civilizing, and Hispanicizing the natives of the region. Missionaries venturing into the wilderness would spread the gospel of Christianity; those Indians converted would be gathered into the missions where Franciscan or Jesuit padres would instruct them. The missionaries would be protected by soldiers, who would be housed in presidios near the religious establishments. The troops would provide the physical strength needed to over-awe the natives, but force would be used only when necessary to coerce the heathens into a receptive attitude toward the teachings of the missionaries. And the families of the soldiers would go with them to the frontier, merchants would come to sell them goods, while farmers and ranchers would be given land in the vicinity. Thus civil settlements, recognized by law, would grow near the presidios and missions. This three-pronged attack on the wilderness, it was felt, would gradually bring the northern frontier under complete Spanish domination and rule.[1]

Missions, Presidios, and Pueblos

When my ancestors came to California in the last half of the Eighteenth Century, they were playing an important role in the expansion of Spain's North American frontier. It was beneficial

---

[1] Odie B. Faulk, "The Presidio: Fortress or Farce?" *Journal of the West*, Vol. VIII, No. 1 (January, 1969), p. 21. Copyright © by *Journal of the West, Inc.*, Reprinted with permission of *Journal of the West*, 1531 Yuma, Manhattan, KS 66502, USA.

SPANISH COLONIAL INSTITUTIONS

for them to become soldiers and take part in this movement because it represented a step up the social and economic ladder in Sinaloa and Sonora.

Spain's plan for the settlement and occupation of Alta California and other frontier territories depended upon three interdependent institutions: the mission, the presidio, and the pueblo (civil settlement). Each of these institutions was considered an essential element in the Spanish conquest of the American Southwest and is discussed separately in the following sections. All three institutions would dominate and guide the lives of my family for several decades.

The Mission

The establishment of the mission in Alta California, according to Dr. Antonio Ríos-Bustamante and Pedro Castillo in *An Illustrated History of Mexican Los Angeles, 1781-1985*, was "viewed even by civil authorities as an important element of frontier settlement:"[2]

> While the primary rationale for the mission system was salvation of heathen souls, Franciscan-run frontier centers also served more earthly objectives: they effectively concentrated and contained potentially hostile Indian people in an environment of

---
[2]Rios-Bustamante and Castillo, *op. cit.*, p. 23.

social indoctrination and acculturation. What's more, they allowed for the formation, training and control of a relatively large Indian labor force capable of producing foodstuffs, materials, and finished products for official purposes. From the perspective of colonial administrators, the ultimate goal of missionization was the incorporation of Indians into colonial society and, ultimately, the conversion of the missions into civil towns.

For their part, Indians saw the missions as places where they could practice adapted religious ceremonies and social activities and work toward the special grace and everlasting life that Christianity promised. Many tribes also sought the opportunity to acquire new material goods (such as iron tolls), agricultural skills, regular meals, and new food stuffs (such as tortillas, beans, fruit, and candies).

The reign of King Carlos III (1759-1788) was one "characterized by a perpetual state of war." Given the widespread military expenditures required to fight the wars and maintain the empire simultaneously, efforts to pacify the northern frontier of Nueva España "had become prohibitively expensive."

For this reason, the Spanish colonial administration decided to turn to the missions as a means of absorbing some of the cost. The cost of the Franciscan missionary settlement was absorbed by the Pious fund, a private endowment.[3]

In some parts of Spain's northern frontier, the mission system was regarded as a dismal failure. Neither the Western Apaches of Arizona nor the Comanches of Texas ever accepted mission life.[4] In fact, at one point, the Apaches "began a vicious and sustained offensive against Spanish and Indian communities and missions of Sonora, Chihuahua, Texas, and New Mexico." So successful were they "that many prosperous ranching and mining areas were completely depopulated and many established towns were either totally destroyed or at least vastly reduced in size."[5]

Nevertheless, the mission system did enjoy some degree of success with the Pimas, Yaquis, and Opatas of Sonora, the Mayos of Sinaloa, the Papagos of Arizona, the Pueblo Indians of New Mexico, and the Hasinai Confederacy of East Texas. However, even the normally acquiescent tribes occasionally rose in rebellion, martyred their missionaries, and burned the religious

---

[3]Daniel J. Garr, *Hispanic Colonial Settlement in California: Planning and Urban Development on the Frontier, 1769-1850.* (Cornell University, Ph.D. Thesis, 1971), pp. 2-3.

[4]Odie B. Faulk, *op. cit.*, p. 21.

[5]Paige W. Christiansen, "The Presidio and the Borderlands: A Case Study," *Journal of the West*, Vol. VIII, No. 1 (January, 1969), p. 29.

SPANISH COLONIAL INSTITUTIONS

establishments. For example, in 1751, the Pimas staged a bloody uprising in their area of Sonora and Arizona."[6]

One of the most serious uprisings took place in August 1680, when all sixty Pueblo villages in present-day New Mexico rose in rebellion. This revolt resulted in the complete expulsion of the Spaniards from Pueblo territory, a situation that continued until 1692. The Pueblos proceeded to methodically rid themselves of every reminder of the Spanish infringement. From 1692 to 1704, the Spaniards embarked upon a campaign of reconquest of all Pueblo territory. As in the other cases of Indian insurrection, the Spanish counterattack turned into a bloody reprisal that subdued the Pueblos once and for all.

In contrast to New Mexico and Arizona, the mission system enjoyed considerable success with the California Indians. Surrounded by some 150,000 California Indians, Father Serra and his successors established twenty-one missions along the California coastline between 1769 and 1823. Each mission was separated by about one day's journey of about forty miles along El Camino Real.

---

[6]Odie B. Faulk, *op. cit.*, p. 21.

SPANISH COLONIAL INSTITUTIONS

Several factors favored the mission development in California: "the missions had unlimited land at their disposal; their Indian converts constituted an abundant labor force; and their padres were talented managers who enjoyed Crown priority in obtaining seeds, plants, implements, and other supplies." During the presidencies of Father Serra (1769-1784) and Father Lasuen (1784-1803), "the missions [in California] had emerged as the main centers of economic activity." Although they depended upon government shipments from San Blas (in the present state of Nayarit) for manufactured articles (clothing and hardware) and some foodstuffs, the missions had, by 1800, been able to produce enough livestock and crops for their subsistence.[7]

The Presidio

In the eyes of the Spanish colonial administrators, the presidio was the most important of the three colonial institutions. Derived from the Latin term *presidium* (a fortified or garrisoned place), the Spanish presidio was seen as an advanced guard of territorial settlement. In a period of thirteen years, four presidios would be founded in Alta California: San Diego (1769), Monterey (1770), San Francisco (1776), and Santa Barbara (1782).

---

[7]Edward F. Staniford, *The Pattern of California History* (New York: Canfield Press, 1975), p. 48.

SPANISH COLONIAL INSTITUTIONS

Choosing a site for the presidio was critical. The site chosen would need to provide maximum advantage against both foreign invasion and Indian attack. In addition, certain rules applied to the construction and design of the presidios. According to the historian Odie B. Faulk, presidios were to be built on high ground and located near good farming land. Built from local materials (usually adobe bricks), the presidios were built in a square or rectangular shape with walls that were at least ten feet high. The length of the sides may have ranged from two to eight hundred feet each. On two diagonal corners, round bastions (toreones) were constructed. The bastions rose above the wall and were pierced with firing ports. Because of this arrangement, soldiers were able to fire down the length of all four walls at attackers.[8]

While the presidios erected by the Spanish forces in Texas, Louisiana, Arizona, New Mexico, and the northern Mexican provinces were primarily "built to control often hostile Indian civilizations," the coastal presidios of California were entrusted with a dual purpose: to pacify the indigenous population and to deter invasions by Spain's European rivals.[9] But life at the California presidios was considerably less dangerous than in those

---

[8]Odie B. Faulk, *op. cit.*, p. 23.

[9]Leon G. Campbell, "The Spanish Presidio in Alta California During the Mission Period 1769-1784," *Journal of the West*, Vol. XVI, No. 4 (October 1977), p. 63.

SPANISH COLONIAL INSTITUTIONS

presidios faced with the threat of Apache or Comanche attacks. In fact, "their tactical strength was never tested, and few battles of consequence were ever fought during the Spanish period" in California.[10]

In the final analysis, Mr. Faulk states that the presidio "could withstand siege, but it could not halt Indian incursions into the interior of New Spain. It served as a refuge during raids for both civilian and soldier, but it rarely was the staging area for a successful campaign against the marauding natives. As a weapon of defense, it was a fortress; as an offensive weapon, it all too often was a farce."[11]

The Pueblo

The presidios and missions essentially paved the way for the establishment of pueblos in Alta California. The original intention was to establish pueblos, which would provide agricultural products at nominal cost and hopefully eliminate the expensive and uncertain journey of the supply ships from San Blas. In the

---

[10]Leon G. Campbell, "The First Californios: Presidial Society in Spanish California, 1769-1822," *Journal of the West*, Vol. XI (October, 1972), p. 583. Reprinted with permission of *Journal of the West*.

[11]Odie B. Faulk, *op. cit.*, p. 27.

opinion of some analysts, the pueblos were, for the most part, a failure:[12]

> The pueblos failed to develop into the thriving, self-supporting agricultural communities based on individual land ownership which had been envisaged by the Crown. For one thing, the Crown recruited settlers from a destitute class of people on the Sinaloa and Sonora frontier. These people lacked the skills, the drive, the substantial means, and the social acceptance to develop into independent farmers. For another thing, the Crown so regulated settler affairs that it stifled much of their initiative in managing their own enterprises. Only a small proportion of settlers developed into enterprising farmers owning their own lands.

Although the short-term goals of the Spanish empire were not met with the establishment of the pueblos, it can be said that the growth of the Los Angeles pueblo – although slow at first – was a success in that it would eventually form the nucleus of a major urban, cultural, and industrial center.

Los Soldados de Cuera

Four of my ancestors originally came to Alta California as *soldados de cuera* (José Rosalino Fernandez, Juan Matias Olivas, Pedro Gabriel Valenzuela, and Anastacio Maria Feliz). And the

---

[12] Edward F. Staniford, *op. cit.*, p. 48.

sons and grandsons of these four pioneers – born, raised and educated within the presidios – followed in the footsteps of their fathers and became soldados. Distinct from Spain's regular soldiers, el soldado de cuera was the standard common soldier of New Spain's northern frontier presidios. He was so-called because of the distinguishing cuera, "a coat of multi-ply buckskin to protect him from the spears and arrows of the enemy."[13] Between 1775 and the time of California's incorporation into the United States, seven of my ancestors would serve as los soldados de cuera in Alta California. The author Max L. Moorhead gives us one description of the difficulties faced by these soldiers:[14]

> It was recognized as far away as Mexico City that the life and service of the soldado de cuera was more strenuous than that of his counterpart in Europe, that he seemed always to be on duty, that he often endured the most inclement weather, and that he suffered intensely from hunger, thirst, and lack of sleep. Quite often he had to put up with a worn-out uniform, damaged weapons, and tired horses. He almost never had time for instruction in his religion, in reading and writing, or even in the military arts on

---

[13]Max L. Moorhead, "The Soldado de Cuera: Stalwart of the Spanish Borderlands" *Journal of the West*, Vol. VIII, No. 1 (January, 1969), p. 38. Copyright © by *Journal of the West, Inc.*, Reprinted with permission of *Journal of the West*, 1531 Yuma, Manhattan, KS 66502, USA.

[14]*Ibid.*, p. 40. Copyright © by *Journal of the West, Inc.*, Reprinted with permission of *Journal of the West*, 1531 Yuma, Manhattan, KS 66502, USA.

which he most depended. With the little solace he gained from the few hours he had with his family, his lot in some respects was worse, and more barbarous than that of the Indians against whom he risked his life in repeated battles.

The cuera worn by the soldiers was inaccurately referred to as a "leather jacket." In fact, it was "a heavy, knee-length, sleeveless coat... made of several thickness of well-cured buckskin (gamuza) bound at the edges with a strong seam and secured to the body of the wearer by encircling straps.... By regulation the cuera contained seven thicknesses of select hides, which officially were considered sufficient to resist the penetration of an Indian arrow, with the outer layer bleached to a uniform whiteness."[15]

"The California soldiery were...", writes the historian Leon G. Campbell, "a tough and hardy breed... well-suited to endure the deprivations of frontier life. Most were men of mestizo, or mixed-blood parentage, recruited from ranchos, villages, and presidios of northern New Spain."[16]

---

[15]*Ibid.*, p. 43.

[16]Leon G. Campbell, "The Spanish Presidio in Alta California During the Mission Period 1769-1784," *op. cit.*, p. 66. Reprinted with permission of *Journal of the West*, 1531 Yuma, Manhattan, KS 66502, USA.

SPANISH COLONIAL INSTITUTIONS

Sidney B. Brinckerhoff and Odie B. Faulk, in *Lancers for the King*, described the "great potential" of this mestizo soldier of northern New Spain:[17]

> In the majority of cases he had been born on that frontier and thus was accustomed to the harsh desert climate and was an expert horseman. He had been so subjected to governmental discipline all his life that he could regard soldiering as the best life available to him. A soldier in the Spanish army had retirement benefits, a pension for his widow in case of his death, and the right to skilled medical attention. There was also the bright hope for promotion... Additionally, the soldier could easily obtain land near the presidio for himself and his family during his 10-year enlistment. The laws also encouraged him to remain permanently on these acres following his discharge. Finally, the soldier had high social standing. His was a vital and necessary function in a society that in actuality was a military hierarchy... Soldiering was an honorable profession.

Mr. Campbell writes that "surviving evidence indicates that on the whole the soldiers were men of good character contrary to the opinion of them held by the friars.... The robustity and individuality of the soldados de cuera, qualities which so admirably suited them for frontier warfare, caused problems in

---

[17]Sidney B. Brinckerhoff and Odie B. Faulk, *Lancers for the King* (Phoenix, Arizona: Arizona Historical Foundation, 1965), pp. 86-87.

their relationships with the priesthood. It seems highly likely that they were sulky and disrespectful to the European-born priests, who probably treated these mixed bloods badly on occasion. The priests feared their irreligiousity in the missions and their sexual appetites for Indian women."[18]

The soldados de cuera were, on average, about thirty-two years of age. In 1773, three-fifths of their number were unmarried. However, within a few years this profile would change dramatically. The Spanish administrators and Catholic priests both favored married soldiers. By 1790, two-thirds of the soldiers in Alta California were married men with families.[19]

The training of soldiers was described in this way: "The captains were expected to drill their men in the handling of fire-arms, in target practice, in mounted tactics, and in military discipline and procedures. Weekly reviews were to be held to inspect equipment and to see that unserviceable items were replaced." But it has been noted that in many cases the regulations were disregarded, and a new soldier had to learn "his profession from his fellow

---

[18]Leon G. Campbell, *op. cit.*, p. 66.

[19]*Ibid.*, p. 66.

enlisted men in barracks discussion or, even worse, on the actual field of battle."[20]

Each leather-jacket soldier was armed with a lance, a short sword with a wide blade (espada ancha), a short-barreled, muzzle-loading rifle (smoothbore), a carbine (escopeta), and a leather shield (adarga). Both the sword and the lance were excellent against an army that stood and fought hand-to-hand, as was traditional in Europe, but useless against Indian attack. Spanish regulations provided that each soldier be issued only three pounds of gunpowder annually. As he was charged for all powder in excess of this amount, he had little interest in target practice.[21]

The adarga was "an oval-shaped bull-hide shield measuring approximately twenty-two inches in height and twenty-five inches in width and weighing four pounds. Although it was capable of warding off an Indian spear or arrow, the adarga, like the cuera, was an impediment to the soldier. He needed at least one hand for his sword, pistol, or lance and another for the reins when he was

---

[20]Odie B. Faulk, *op. cit.*, p. 23; "Distribution of Funds and the Pay of Soldiers," in the Royal Regulations as quoted in Brinckerhoff and Faulk, *Lancers for the king*, pp. 23-25.

[21]Odie B. Faulk, *op. cit.*, pp. 26-27; Paige W. Christiansen, *op. cit.*, p. 29;"Armament and Mounts," in the Royal Regulations as quoted in Brinckerhoff and Faulk, *Lancers for the king*, pp. 21-22.

on horseback. When dismounted he needed both hands for his musket."[22] In the final analysis, Max L. Moorhead gives us this description of the soldado de cuera:[23]

> Although he was untrained in the formal military arts and woefully lacking in discipline, he brought to the service a stamina, spirit, and peculiar talent which Indian fighting demanded and which Spanish regulars usually lacked. Although recruited from the rustic society of the frontier, often from the illiterate lower castes, he rose through the ranks to positions of command. He had more military assignments to carry out than time permitted. Every year he spent months on campaign into waterless deserts, weeks on short rations, days in the saddle, nights without sleep, and hours in mortal combat. He was overly burdened by armor and weapons, and these were seldom in serviceable condition. He had to buy, repair, and replace these from his own salary, and this was all too small.

---

[22]Max L. Moorhead, *op. cit.*, p. 45.

[23]*Ibid.*, p. 53. Copyright © by *Journal of the West, Inc.*, Reprinted with permission of *Journal of the West*, 1531 Yuma, Manhattan, KS 66502, USA.

THE FOUNDING OF SAN DIEGO

> San Diego considers itself the "birthplace of California." It was the first part of what is now the state of California to be explored by Europeans, and the first to be colonized. Although San Diego was not settled by Europeans as early as were many East Coast areas, its history is at least as rich. Home to four major cultures (Indian, Spanish, Mexican, American), a succession of explorers, missionaries, governors, overland traders, and land promoters all arrived here early and left their marks, nearly eliminating in the process the Native Americans who had known the land for centuries before.[1]

The Expeditions of 1769

The four expeditions of 1769 were united in San Diego on July 1, 1769. On July 16, the *Mission San Diego de Alcalá* was founded, to be followed in the next 54 years by a chain of twenty more missions stretching northward through Alta California to present-day Sonoma. The mission was ceremonially established by the erection of a cross and celebration of mass on a great hillside overlooking the ocean.

The party attempted to attract the attention of local Indians by hanging bells in the trees and putting out token gifts. However, the local Indians, described as "too clever, wide-awake and

---

[1] Philip R. Pryde (ed.), *San Diego: An Introduction to the Region* (Dubuque, Iowa: Kendall/Hunt Publishing Co., 1976), p. 5.

THE FOUNDING OF SAN DIEGO

business-like for any Spaniard to get ahead of them," attacked the mission in the first month.[2]

On July 14, 1769, Portola had left San Diego, on his expedition to Monterey, with a force of sixty-four men, including twenty-seven *soldados de cuera* (leather-jacket soldiers) under Captain Fernando Rivera. On August 2, 1769, they camped alongside a river which they named *Nuestra Señora de Los Angeles de Porciúncula* (Our Lady of the Angels of the Porciúncula). The river's name was soon shortened to Porciúncula ("Little Portion"). Today we know the Porciúncula as the Los Angeles River.

The Indians in this area lived in huts of woven tules that resembled gigantic beehives and lived off of edible roots, acorns, wild sage, and berries. Armed only with stone-tipped sticks, the Indians gathered around the strange pale-faced visitors and tried to exchange their woven baskets for beads.[3] An Indian village called *Yang-na* stood in the area of the present City Hall. According to Father Juan Crespí, who was a member of the expedition, "all the requisites for a large settlement" could be found in this area. He

---

[2] Daniel J. Garr, op. cit., p. 94.

[3] Regina V. Phelan, *The Land Known as Alta California* (Spokane, WA: Prosperity Press, 1997), p. 4.

THE FOUNDING OF SAN DIEGO

noted "a large vineyard of wild grapes" and "an infinity of rose bushes in full bloom." He also pronounced the soil to be "capable of producing every kind of grain and fruit."[4] It was on this site that the pueblo of Los Angeles would be founded twelve years later. On September 8, 1771, the San Gabriel Mission was founded nine miles east of this site along the *Rio de Jesus de los Temblores* (River of Earthquakes). This mission would become an important junction from which expeditions to Los Angeles and Santa Barbara would extend.

San Diego

In 1774, the San Diego Mission was moved across and up the valley six miles inland to a better location in Mission Valley. The San Diego Presidio, with a military force of thirty men, remained on the commanding hillside. By December 31, 1774, the San Diego Mission and Presidio had nineteen families with a total of ninety-seven persons. During these early years, relations with the local Indians remained very poor, and on the night of November 5, 1775, approximately six hundred Indians attacked and burned the mission to the ground.

---

[4] W.W. Robinson, *Los Angeles: From the Days of the Pueblo* (Revised: North Hollywood: California Historical Society, 1981), p. 16.

THE FOUNDING OF SAN DIEGO

With hostile Indians on the outside, and a scarcity of supplies arriving from San Blas, life was – at best – difficult. According to Iris Engstrand, in *Serra's San Diego: Father Junipero Serra and California's Beginnings*:[5] "Rations were always scarce and the wives of soldiers made tortillas from the small supply of corn for their own families and the single men. Beans and sometimes a little fish or meat supplemented the meager diet. Crops were planted near the river with hopes for more abundant provisions."

According to the garrison roster of December 21, 1777, the *soldado de cuera* Anastasio Feliz was listed as one of the forty-eight privates stationed at San Diego.[6] Anastasio is my great-great-great-great-great-great-great-grandfather and is believed to have been my first ancestor from Mexico to reach California, possibly as early as 1774.

Felipe de Neve

When Felipe de Neve (1727-1784) was appointed the Governor of California in March 1775, the capital of the "Californias" was at Loreto in Baja California. However, on February 3, 1777, when

---

[5] Iris H.W. Engstrand, op. cit., p. 11.

[6] Bill Mason, "The Garrisons of San Diego Presidio: 1770-1794," *The Journal of San Diego History*, Vol. XXIV, No. 4 (Fall, 1978), pp. 405-406.

THE FOUNDING OF SAN DIEGO

de Neve took office, Monterey became the capital of both Alta California and Baja California, symbolizing the new importance of the northern province. By this time, eight of the 21 missions had already been established. In those days, the only way supplies could reach the Spanish outposts and missions in Alta California was by ships out of far away San Blas.

After a tour of California, Governor de Neve proposed to the colonial administrators that, in order to further secure Alta California as a Spanish possession, it would be necessary to create agricultural sites. The products of these farming communities would help relieve California's dependence on ship-borne imports of foodstuffs from San Blas. To do this, de Neve stated that he would need to import settlers from the northern provinces of Nueva España to cultivate the fields. Upon this recommendation, Spanish colonial authorities decided to establish a new pueblo in the southern part of Alta California between San Diego and San José.

THE EXPEDITION OF 1781

As some of the members of this famous expedition were the founders and first settlers of the City of Los Angeles, it becomes a matter of historical importance to know who and what they were, whence they came and the imprint they left upon the land of their adoption. True, not all of them were Spaniards, but they sprang from hardy stock, and the blood of true Pioneers coursed through their veins. For it took not only the spirit of adventure, but stout hearts as well, to leave their friends and firesides in those sleepy valleys of Sonora and Sinaloa, and test their fortunes "en la California Septentrional," where under the "Seven stars," they were to found a Pueblo, today one of the metropolises of the world.[1]

The Search for Recruits

In December 1779, Governor de Neve sent an expedition under the command of Captain Fernando Rivera into Sinaloa and Sonora to recruit 59 soldiers and 24 families of *pobladores* (settlers). Of the fifty-nine recruits, thirty-four soldiers were to go to California, while the other twenty-five would fill the places of those soldiers taken from the presidios in Mexico.[2]

The instructions required that the soldier recruits and the settlers should be "healthy, robust, and without known vice or defect." Both the soldiers and settlers were to be married men – with

---

[1] Thomas Workman Temple II, "Soldiers and Settlers of the Expedition of 1781," *Southern California Quarterly*, Vol. XV, Part 1 (November 1931), p. 99.

[2] Robert S. Whitehead, *Citadel on the Channel: The Royal Presidio of Santa Barbara: Its Founding and Construction, 1782-1798* (Santa Barbara: Santa Barbara Trust for Historical Preservation, 1996), pp. 60-61.

THE EXPEDITION OF 1781

families – and should possess "greater strength and endurance for the hardships of frontier service." Included among the settlers would be a mason, a carpenter, and a blacksmith. Rivera was to offer prospective colonists daily rations and a monthly salary of 10 pesos for the next three years, as well as "an allowance in clothing and supplies." The settlers would be granted the use of government land as common pasture and would also be granted an exemption from taxes for five years.[3]

All recruits were required to bind themselves to ten years' service. It was also hoped that the unmarried female relatives of the pobladores would be encouraged to marry bachelor soldiers already in California. Upon completion of his task, Rivera would assemble the whole company of recruits at Álamos in Sonora. From Álamos the recruits and their families would move on by sea or land. In addition to recruiting soldiers and settlers, Rivera had to purchase equipment and supplies, as well as 961 horses, mules,

---

[3] Marion Parks, "Instructions for the Recruital of Soldiers and Settlers for California – Expedition of 1781," *Southern California Quarterly*, Vol. XV, Part II (1931), pp. 189-203; Thomas Workman Temple II, "Se Fundaron un Púeblo de Espanoles, The Founding of Los Angeles," *Southern California Quarterly*, Vol. XV, Part 1 (November 1931), pp. 78-79.

THE EXPEDITION OF 1781

and donkeys. The animals would be sent north by way of the Gila and Colorado Rivers.[4]

Although he started his search in February 1780, Rivera did not enlist his first settler until May. It was difficult to enlist people for a ten-year commitment to a remote and desolate outpost surrounded by thousands of potentially hostile Indians. Most people realized that getting to California from Sonora and Sinaloa was a long, arduous and dangerous journey. Additionally, rumors were circulating in Sonora that soldiers serving in California were not getting paid their due.

By August 1, 1780, Rivera had recruited only 45 soldiers and seven settlers from Sinaloa and Culiacán. But, by August 25, he was able to recruit eleven farm families (numbering 44 people in all) and 59 soldiers.[5] By November, Captain Rivera had recruited all of the soldiers he needed, but was still short on settlers.

---

[4] Robert S. Whitehead, *op. cit.*, p. 61.

[5] Meredith Stevens, *The House of Olivas* (Ventura, California: Charon Press), p. 27; "Se Fundaron un Púeblo de Espanoles," *op. cit.*, p. 80.

THE EXPEDITION OF 1781

The Expedition

Rivera's entire expedition of settlers, soldiers, and livestock were assembled at Álamos in January. At this point, he decided to split the expedition into two groups. First, he assigned seventeen of his soldiers under the command of Lieutenant José de Zuñiga to accompany the eleven settlers' families in their march up the Baja Peninsula.

This party – which included my eighth great-grandfather Luis Quintero and his family – left Álamos on February 2, 1781, started northward, and eventually crossed the Gulf of California from Guaymas to Loreto, Baja California. An outbreak of smallpox among the settlers delayed the journey. Some of the settlers headed north on March 12th, while a second group did not proceed until May 16th.

The settlers stopped briefly at the San Diego Presidio before moving on to the San Gabriel Mission where they arrived on August 18, 1781 after a journey of 950 miles. At that point, the settlers were only nine miles from their destination (Los Angeles), but had to be quarantined for 17 days at a short distance from the mission because of exposure to smallpox.[6]

---

[6] Bancroft, *California*, I, pp. 340-345; Robert S. Whitehead, *op. cit.*, p. 64; "Se Fundaron un Púeblo de Espanoles," *op. cit.*, pp. 81-85.

THE EXPEDITION OF 1781

The second part of the expedition did not leave Álamos until April 1781. At that time, Rivera started out with forty-two soldiers and thirty families. No settlers took part in this movement as the soldiers, with the wives, children, and livestock in tow, traveled the long, arduous overland route through desert brush and hostile Indian territory. Progress was quite slow, in accordance with their directive, to avoid needless fatigue and hardship to the families, and to keep the livestock in good condition.

Rivera and his troops arrived in July at the junction of the Gila and Colorado Rivers. At that point, Rivera sent the troops and their families ahead to the San Gabriel Mission. With several men still under his command, Rivera camped on the eastern (Arizona) bank of the Colorado on the night of July 17, 1781 in order to rest and feed his livestock before crossing the Colorado Desert. However, Rivera's large herd of cattle and horses caused a great deal of damage to the Indians' mesquite trees and melon patches. Enraged, the Yuma Indians attacked and massacred Rivera and several of his soldiers. At the same time, the Indians also attacked two nearby pueblos, killing a total of 46 people.[7]

---

[7] Charles Chapman, *op. cit.*, pp. 330-342; Robert S. Whitehead, *op. cit.*, p. 65.

THE EXPEDITION OF 1781

Fortunately, the thirty-five soldiers and thirty families of the Sonora escort had already arrived safely at the San Gabriel Mission on July 14, 1781. This massacre caused a great deal of trepidation to the Spanish frontier zone. As a result the inland route from Sonora to California was virtually closed for several years.

On the following page we have reproduced a map – prepared through courtesy of Phil Townsend Hanna and the "Touring Topics" – showing the two routes taken by the soldiers and settlers in the Expedition of 1781.[8]

Among *los soldados de cuera* in the Expedition of 1781 was my ancestor, 21-year-old Juan Matias Olivas from Rosario, Sinaloa. Juan Matias was accompanied on the expedition by his wife, Dorotea Barbara Espinosa, and two infant children, María Nicolasa and José Pablo. While Juan Matias Olivas was assigned to accompany the settlers on their overland journey, the recently married Pedro Gabriel Valenzuela, a soldado de cuera from Álamos, and his young bride, María Dolores Parra, accompanied Rivera on his journey north.

---

[8] Reproduced from the *Historical Society of Southern California Quarterly* (1931).

THE EXPEDITION OF 1781

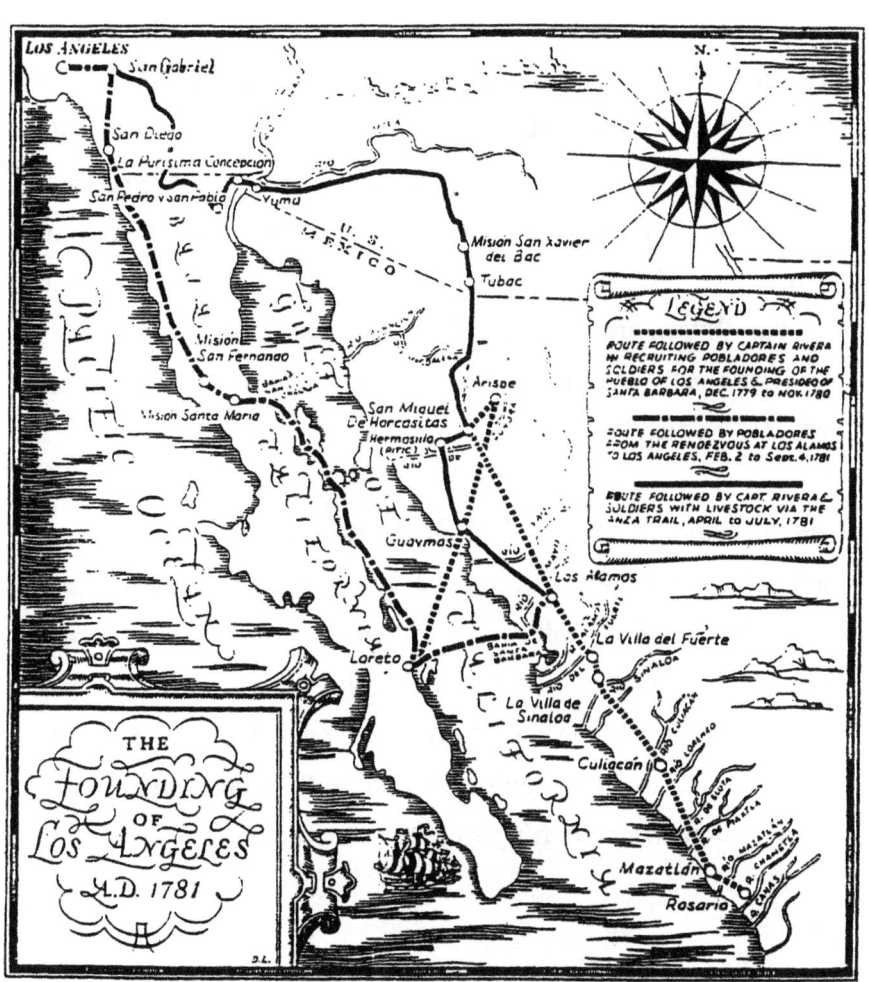

The Expedition of 1781
©*Historical Society of Southern California Quarterly (1931)*

THE EXPEDITION OF 1781

Riding alongside Pedro Gabriel Valenzuela on the expedition was another soldado named José Rosalino Fernández. Months earlier, Fernández had married María Juana Josefa Quintero, a daughter of one of the eleven settlers, Luis Quintero. The young couple brought with them their first-born child, María Luciana Fernández, who would marry the first-born son of Juan Matias Olivas ninteen years later. All three soldiers – Pedro Gabriel Valenzuela, Juan Matias Olivas, and José Rosalino Fernández – are my ancestors and were listed in a roster of soldiers stationed at the San Gabriel Mission on October 4, 1781.[9]

As they traveled northward during the middle months of 1781, my ancestors could not have imagined that someday the small pueblo they were about to build would become one of the largest urban, cultural and economic centers of the world. To them, this was merely a risky undertaking designed to plant a colony of Spanish-speaking settlers in the midst of a potentially hostile environment located along the outer fringes of the Spanish empire.

---

[9] *Provincial State Papers*, Benicia Military, II, pp. 60-63.

THE FOUNDING OF LOS ANGELES

Few of the great cities of the land have had such humble founders as Los Angeles. Of the eleven pobladores who built their huts of poles and tule thatch around the plaza vieja ... not one could read or write. Not one could boast of an unmixed ancestry... the conquering race that possesses the land they colonized has forgotten them. No street or landmark in the city bears the name of any one of them[1]

These first settlers were very brave. They had traveled over many miles of desert to start the pueblo. They had many, many hardships... They were the pioneers who cleared the fields and used the water from the river to make things grow.... The jobs were done without many of the things that people now have to make their work easy... They had no railroads, airplanes, automobiles, telephones, postal service, newspapers, books, magazines, motion pictures, and radios to help them.[2]

The Founding of Los Angeles

On the morning of September 4, 1781, forty-four persons set out from the San Gabriel Mission with an escort of soldiers and priests. It is said that Governor de Neve led the people in a parade, followed first by the soldiers and padres, who were then followed by the settlers. The travelers carried their belongings on their backs or upon their mules as they crossed the Los Angeles River. By late afternoon, the party arrived at the site of their new

---

[1] J. M. Guinn, *Historical and Biographical Record of Los Angeles and Vicinity* (Chicago: Chapman Publishing Co., 1901), p. 32.

[2] Gertrude Van Aken, *El Pueblo Under The Spanish Flag* (Los Angeles: Office of the Superintendent, Los Angeles city Schools, 1946), pp. 16-17.

THE FOUNDING OF LOS ANGELES

home. Ceremonies were concluded by prayers and blessings from the padres, shortly after which, the flag of Our Lady of the Angels was raised over *El Pueblo de Nuestra la Reina de Los Angeles del Rio Porciúncula*. In *The Land Known as Alta California*, the author Regina V. Phelan described the first night at the new pueblo:[3]

> That evening the women fetched water from the river and cooked supper for their families. The older boys took care of the livestock. The girls quieted their baby brothers and sisters. The men set about marking off their small parcels of land, then started building earthen-roofed huts of willow branches interlaced with tules gathered from the river.

Some researchers have suggested that the founding of the Pueblo may have been a more gradual process and that this grand procession on September 4th may not have taken place as dramatized by some historians. The one thing that is certain is that there is very little documentation about the first years of the pueblo and the events that took place there.

Of the fourteen pobladores that had been enlisted, only eleven of them – with their families – actually took part in the founding of

---

[3] Regina V. Phelan, op. cit., p. 22-23.

THE FOUNDING OF LOS ANGELES

the Pueblo of Los Angeles. A list of the first settlers, as indicated by a *padrón* (census) taken on November 19, 1781, is shown below. This listing – which groups together people of the same surname – can also be found on the *Pobladores'* plaque on the south side of Pueblo Plaza in Downtown Los Angeles:[4]

Lara
José Fernanco de, Español, Hombre, 50
María Antonio, India, Mujer, 23
María Juan, Niña, 6
José Julian, Niño, 4
María Faustina, Niña, 2

Navarro
José Antonio, Mestizo, Hombre, 42
María Regina, Mulata, Mujer, 47
José Eduardo, Niño, 10
José Clemente, Niño, 9
Mariana, Niña, 4

Rosas
Basilio, Indio, Hombre, 67
María Manuela, Mulata, Mujer, 43
José Maxímo, Niño, 15
José Carlos, Niño, 12
María Josefa, Niña, 8
Antonio Rosalino, Niño, 7
José Marcelino, Niño, 4
José Esteban, Niño, 2

---

[4] Provincial State Papers, Missions and Colonization, To. 1, pp. 101-102.

THE FOUNDING OF LOS ANGELES

Mesa
Antonio, Negro, Hombre, 38
María Ana, Mulata, Mujer, 27
María Paula, Niña, 10
Antonio María, Niño, 8

Villavicencio
Antonio Clemente, Español, Hombre, 30
María Seferina, India, Mujer, 26
María Antonia, Niña, 8

Vanegas
José, Indio, Hombre, 28
María Bonifacia, India, Mujer, 20
Cosme Damien, Niño, 1

Rosas
Alejandro, Indio, Hombre, 19
Juana María, India, Mujer, 20

Rodríguez
Pablo, Indio, Hombre, 25
María Rosalía, India, 26
María Antonia, Niña, 1

Camero
Manuel, Mulato, Hombre, 30
María Tomasa, Mulata, Mujer, 24

Quintero
Luis, Negro, Hombre, 55
María Petra, Mulata, Mujer, 40
María Gertrudis, Niña, 16
María Concepcíon, Niña, 9
María Tomasa, Niña, 7

THE FOUNDING OF LOS ANGELES

María Rafaela, Niña, 6
José Clemente, Niño, 3

Moreno
José, Mulato, Hombre, 22
María Guadalupe, Mulata, Mujer, 19

The Spanish racial classifications used to describe the settlers were used throughout the Spanish Empire. *Español* indicated a person of Spanish descent, while the term *indio/india* simply implied the male and female genders for *Indian*. A *mestizo* usually indicated a person of half Spanish and half Indian blood, while a *mulato* or *mulata* indicated a person of mixed African and Spanish origins. The *Negro* classification of my ancestor Luis Quintero generally indicates a person of predominantly African heritage.

The new pueblo was six miles square with a plaza near its center. Each family was given a small piece of land, in addition to receiving two mares, two cows, one calf, two sheep, two goats, two mules, and two oxen, as well as implements with which to work the land. They had five years to pay for these items.[5] All of the settlers also had access to an anvil, a forge, six crowbars, six

---

[5] Gertrude Van Aken, *op. cit.*, pp. 12-13.

iron spades, tools for carpentry and cast work, some carts, and wagons.[6]

After the initial settlement of the pueblo, there was a great deal of work yet to be done. For that reason it is possible that some of the soldiers – many of whom were destined for service at the proposed Santa Barbara Presidio – had new responsibilities. According to Meredith Stevens, "The soldiers remained there to help the settlers get established. They built pole and mud huts with earthen roofs, and made corrals of willow poles laced with rawhide. They dug wells, cleared land for planting and set up an irrigation system fed from the river by *zanja madre* (mother ditch). After eight months of exhausting labor, in April 1782, the little village was crudely completed and most of the soldiers were sent north to build the new presidio at Santa Barbara."[7]

The primary purpose for building the *zanja madre* was agricultural. From this main ditch, smaller ditches branched off to be used for irrigation of crops in different sectors. However, the smaller ditches were also used for drinking water and laundering. People in town went to the nearest ditch to fill their *ollas* (clay

---

[6] Regina V. Phelan, op. cit., p. 22.

[7] Meredith Stevens, op. cit., p. 29.

THE FOUNDING OF LOS ANGELES

water jugs). A man called a *zanjero* was paid to watch the ditch and make sure that the cattle, sheep, and horses were kept out of the open ditches.[8]

For the rest of 1781, as the Quintero family stayed at the Pueblo, the Fernandez, Olivas and Valenzuela families were quartered with the other soldiers' families at the San Gabriel Mission. The establishment of the Santa Barbara Presidio scheduled for 1781 had to be postponed. Governor de Neve delayed this mission until the spring because of transportation issues and the rainy season.[9]

---

[8] Gertrude Van Aken, op. cit., pp. 23-24.

[9] Robert S. Whitehead, *op.cit.*, p. 65.

SANTA BARBARA

The founding of the Presidio of Santa Barbara and the Pueblo of Los Angeles made the colonial organization of California complete. The basic structure on which military control, colonial occupation and missionary endeavor were to advance from this time on was established. The Province was divided into four presidial districts, of which Santa Barbara was second. Its jurisdiction extended over the region ultimately occupied by the five missions of Santa Barbara, La Purisima Conception, Santa Ines, San Buenaventura and San Fernando and the Pueblo of Los Angeles...

For soldiers and missionaries alike, it was easier to get to California than to obtain permission or means to get away. Salaries were small in all ranks... Even in the Presidio of Santa Barbara, where circumstances were favorable, the first decade was in truth a time of pioneering, full of work and want, with no luxuries and sparse comforts.[1]

Santa Barbara

While the pobladores got down to the business of developing their small pueblo along the Los Angeles River, most of the *soldados de cuera* from the Expedition of 1781 stayed at San Gabriel to prepare for their next assignment. In his edict of 1774, King Carlos had referred to the foundation of a Santa Barbara presidio as an "indispensable" element for the protection of Alta California.

---

[1] Owen H. O'Neill (ed.), *History of Santa Barbara County: Its People and Resources* (Santa Barbara: Harold MacLean Meier, 1939), pp. 52-53.

SANTA BARBARA

With this objective in mind, the Santa Barbara Company at San Gabriel anxiously prepared for the establishment of the new presidio, as well as missions at both San Buenaventura and Santa Barbara.

Santa Barbara lies along the Pacific Ocean almost 100 miles northwest of Los Angeles. In those days, the Santa Monica Mountains, Tehachapi Mountains, and the San Gabriel-San Bernardino Mountain range represented a formidable barrier to north-south travel for Spaniard and Indian alike.

Southeast of present-day Santa Barbara, the Santa Monica Mountains drop off abruptly into the Pacific Ocean. Armed expeditions seeking to travel through the area northward to Monterey had to thread their way carefully along the coastal Indian trails in the beach area. During the winter rainy season, the route was almost impassable for horses and mules.

According to Monsignor Francis J. Weber in his work, *Queen of the Missions*, the purpose for establishing the Santa Barbara Presidio was to "hold California together." He went on to explain that "Felipe de Neve... saw that the Santa Barbara Channel was a danger spot. There the mountains came right down to the sea. Any road cutting through the area would have to run closer to the shoreline. And if the large Indian population should rise to revolt, the narrow passage might easily be blocked and California would be cut in half. The bond between San Diego and the two northern presidios would be severed." For this reason, de Neve took steps to establish three missions and one presidio along the Santa Barbara Channel in a very short period of time. The presidio and the missions, together, would thus "establish a firm bond of unity between north and south."[2]

However, heavy rains during the Autumn and Winter of 1781/1782, delayed the expedition until the Spring. As a result, the Santa Barbara Company was ordered to remain at the San Gabriel Mission, where the soldiers and their families were housed in forty small palisade huts with flat roofs. Lieutenant José Francisco Ortega (1734-1798), Commander of the garrison at the San Diego Presidio since 1773, was appointed commander of the Santa Barbara Company and started to organize and train the unit for its new assignment. Lieutenant Ortega was a native of Celaya in present-day state of Guanajuato and had enlisted in the service in 1755.[3]

---

[2] Msgr. Francis J. Weber (ed.), *Queen of the Missions: A Documentary History of Santa Barbara* (Hong Kong: Libra Press, Limited, 1979), p. 26.

[3] Robert S. Whitehead, *op. cit.*, pp. 66, 69; *Provincial State Papers*, Benicia Military, III, p. 302.

SANTA BARBARA

An initial list of the soldiers who would garrison the presidio and missions along the Santa Barbara Channel was prepared on October 30, 1781 by Lieutenant Ortega at San Gabriel. The garrison of seven officers and fifty-four soldiers included Anastasio María Feliz, Rosalino Fernández, and Juan Matias Olivas – all of whom are my ancestors. By this time, seven privates and a corporal had been withdrawn from each of the companies of the Monterey and San Diego presidios as a cadre to help train the recruits.

With several years of experience behind him, Anastasio Feliz – who had been stationed at San Diego, Tubac (Nogales), and Monterey – was dispatched to San Gabriel as part of the cadre. In the meantime, Pedro Gabriel Valenzuela – a soldier with less experience on the California frontier – was transferred to the San Diego Presidio, ostensibly to replace one of the departing soldiers at that presidio.

By February 1782, the hostilities that took place on the Colorado River the previous summer had subsided, and Governor de Neve made the decision to proceed with the founding of the Channel establishments. Soon, Father Serra traveled from Monterey to San

SANTA BARBARA

Gabriel to be a part of this event, arriving at the Mission on March 19, 1782.[4]

On March 26, the Santa Barbara Company consisting of fifty-seven officers and men under the command of Lieutenant Ortega finally left San Gabriel. The entire expedition numbered some 200 people and included about 200 horses and mules. In addition to the soldiers, the Governor, ten soldiers from the Monterrey Company, muleteers with trains of utensils and food supplies, Indian auxiliaries, and the wives and children of the soldiers formed the large procession.[5]

On March 29, 1782, the Santa Barbara Company reached San Buenaventura where the ninth Alta California mission was founded by Father Serra. On Eastern Sunday, March 31, Father Serra performed his first Mass at this site. "Immediately after the founding ceremonies," writes Mr. Whitehead, "the soldiers, with the help of the Indians from the adjacent village of *Shisholop*, began constructing the palisade-type mission."[6]

---

[4] Robert S. Whitehead, *op. cit.*, p. 67; Father Maynard J. Geiger (trans.), *Palóu's Life of Fray Junipero Serra* (Washington, 1955), p. 220.

[5] *Ibid.*, pp. 220-221; Robert S. Whitehead, *op. cit.*, pp. 76-77

[6] *Ibid.*, p. 77.

121

SANTA BARBARA

The entire expedition became involved in the construction of the chapel and dwelling places during the next two weeks. On April 24, 1782, Governor de Neve was able to report to his superior officer that the Mission of San Buenaventura had been completed, indicating that the natives of the region were pleased with the presence of the settlement.[7]

On April 15, 1782, Governor de Neve assembled forty-two soldiers to resume the expedition toward Santa Barbara. Sergeant Pablo Antonio Cota and fourteen soldiers were left in San Buenaventura to protect the mission and to continue with the building.[8] The expedition marched twenty-seven miles along the coast between the Pacific Ocean and the high cliffs flanking the shoreline. For much of the first ten miles, the soldiers had to walk through the surf at the base of the cliffs. They found several Indian villages along the way.[9]

---

[7] *Ibid.*, pp. 80-81; Provincial Record, II, 277-279.

[8] *Provincial State Papers*, Benicia Military, III, pp. 106-108; Robert S. Whitehead, *op. cit.*, p. 81.

[9] *Ibid.*, p. 81.

SANTA BARBARA

The Company crossed the Rincon Creek and entered the Valley of Carpinteria. Passing around a lagoon, they found a good-sized Indian village ruled over by a friendly Indian chief, Yanonali. From April 15th – the day they arrived – to April 21st, Governor de Neve and Lieutenant Ortega surveyed the entire area to decide the best location for the new presidio.

The eventual site decided upon "was chosen because of distance from the main Indian village, proximity to the lagoon, elevation above surrounding land which provided a view of incoming ships and possible attack by hostile Indians, good drainage in wet weather and because it was close enough to shore for transporting supplies delivered by ship yet far enough away to be out of the cannon-reach of enemy ships."[10]

The joint ceremonies, conducted by Governor de Neve and Father Serra at Santa Barbara on Sunday, April 21, 1782, were described by the historian, Walter A. Hawley in *The Early Days of Santa Barbara*.[11]

> The soldiers, with faces bronzed by exposure and clad in leathern waistcoasts and leggings, were

---

[10] *Ibid.*, pp. 82-89.

[11] Walter A. Hawley, *The Early Days of Santa Barbara* (Santa Barbara Heritage, 1987, 3rd edition), pp. 45-46.

SANTA BARBARA

assembled near the intersection of Canon Perdido and Santa Barbara streets... From the many rancherías throughout the valleys the Indians had come, impelled by curiosity and awe; and it must have been with interest that they watched the newcomers and wondered at their purpose.

Father Junipero, clad in alb and stole, stood in a hastily constructed chapel of brush before a roughly hewn table used as an altar. The soldiers, under the command of Governor Neve and Captain Ortega, then formed a square, and having laid aside their shields and lances, knelt with bare heads while the reverend Father with uplifted hands invoked the blessings of heaven upon the congregation and their undertaking. After the dedication of the spot, the cross was raised, mass was celebrated, and an impressive sermon was preached. With these simple ceremonies was founded the City of Santa Barbara.

As forty-two soldados stood by, Governor Neve took possession of the site in the name of King Carlos III of Spain. I am proud to say that many of my ancestors stood as witnesses to this event. Juan Matias Olivas, Jose Rosalino Fernandez, and Anastacio Feliz – all of whom are my great-great-great-great-great-great-great-grandfathers – were present, along with their families. It is believed that Rosalino Fernandez's wife, Maria Josefa Quintero, and her parents, Luis Quintero and Maria Petra Rubio – my eighth great-grandparents – were also present at this ceremony. Luis had been one of the founders of the Los Angeles Pueblo but – for reasons to be discussed in the next chapter – was now destined to be among the founders of Santa Barbara.

In the days and weeks to follow, the soldiers set about their task of building the presidio by cutting down nearby oak trees in order to build the 165-foot square enclosure. The best description of the responsibilities of the soldiers and their families has been provided by Meredith Stevens in *The House of Olivas*:[12]

> The men cleared the area, constructed rawhide corrals and crude shelters for the horses and other livestock, and established a campsite. Two wells were dug for their water supply, and these wells would one day be within the military compound along with a cistern to conserve the water. Then the process of producing adobe bricks was begun, a process which would continue throughout the construction period. The first structure to be erected was the exterior wall. Once that was completed they could begin on the storehouses, living quarters and the chapel. Construction would require four years....
>
> While the men labored on the building, the women were far from idle. They did the cooking, saw to the laundry, sewed, knitted and tended the children, although generally the older girl children were charged with caring for the younger ones. Even

---

[12] Meredith Stevens, *op. cit.*, pp. 33-34.

when the presidio was completed, living conditions were far from lavish. One room was allotted to married soldiers and their families, and this was only for sleeping purposes. The furnishings of these rooms consisted primarily of beds, which were made of hide springs on a wood frame supporting mattresses made of wool or feathers... Even after the construction period, cooking and laundry continued to be done by the women. Carding, spinning wool weaving, and making soap and candles were also activities of the women, as was ironing, which was done by pressing with the hand until the cloth was smooth.

To the dismay of Father Serra, Governor de Neve refused permission for the building of the mission until the construction of the presidio could be finished. Feeling uneasy about the large Indian population in the area, de Neve felt that the fortifications should be built and the security of the presidio guaranteed before any construction began on the Mission. Regrettably, Father Serra died on August 28, 1784 in Monterey before the Santa Barbara Mission was established.

The next four years at the Santa Barbara Presidio were years of adjustment to frontier living. The soldiers and their families had to learn from the Indians how to live off the land and existed on a starvation diet of only 1,200 calories a day. The life of the presidial soldier involved much more than building the presidio or

SANTA BARBARA

standing guard along the fortress garrison. Meredith Stevens described in detail some of these duties:[13]

> In 1786, a "Royal Rancho" was established, a beef raising rancho, which would provide food for the presidio. So in addition to manning the presidio and the four missions [Santa Barbara, San Buenaventura, La Purísima Concepción, and San Luis Obispo] the soldiers were also the vaqueros who manned the rancho, tended livestock and mended fences, etc. The presidio provided guards for the little farming community of Los Angeles as well. Other duties of the soldiers included carrying mail and escorting pack trains sent to Los Angeles for provisions... Soldiers also served as escorts for any sort of official entourage. Additionally, individual soldiers apparently raised some crops on their own, for they hired Indian boys to keep birds away from their fields.

At the end of 1782, Lieutenant Ortega penned his year-end strength report required of all Spanish companies. In addition to himself and five other officers, fifty soldiers were stationed at the Santa Barbara Presidio. However, of the fifty soldiers officially serving at the presidio, fifteen were in the *escolta* (soldier escort) at San Buenaventura, seven at San Luis Obispo on temporary assignment, and two were in Los Angeles. This left a force of thirty-two men at the presidio, ostensibly to defend a two hundred

---

[13] *Ibid.*, pp. 38-39.

mile coastline between Los Angeles and Morro Bay from attack by hostile Indians or foreign invaders.[14] By December 1783, the garrison at the presidio had increased only slightly to 58 men.[15] By the end of 1785, the total population of the presidio had increased to 203, of which forty-seven were women.[16]

Lieutenant Ortega, a close friend of Father Serra, had been assigned the task of making contact with the neighboring Indian tribes. According to Monsignor Weber, "his instructions were precise and detailed. He was to contact the headmen of the various Indian villages and explain the presence of the Spanish in their midst. He was to make clear that the Spanish had come to populate the land, to take the Indians under their protection, to live with them in love and friendship, to defend them against their enemies, and to teach them to know and love God. This message was to be accompanied by kindness, gentleness, good treatment, and gifts."[17]

---

[14] Robert S. Whitehead, *op. cit.*, p. 98; *Provincial State Papers*, Benicia Military, IV, p. 159.

[15] *Provincial State Papers. Presidios*, p. 7.

[16] *Provincial State Papers. Missions*, I, pp. 5-10.

[17] Monsignor Francis J. Weber (ed.), *op. cit.*, p. 26.

SANTA BARBARA

The Chumash Indians who inhabited the area around the Santa Barbara Presidio were very numerous. Along the coastline they had some forty-one villages between the San Buenaventura and Point Concepción. Fifteen more villages were to be found on the Channel Islands off the coast. The Chumash sustained themselves by hunting, fishing and seed-gathering. They were described as "affable and gentle, liberal and hospitable to strangers, agile and alert, lively, industrious, skillful and clever." Because of their friendly and helpful nature, the Chumash became active participants in the construction of the presidio.[18]

In 1784, Lieutenant Ortega was succeeded as Comandant of the Santa Barbara Presidio by Captain Felipe de Goycoechea (1747-1814), who held the position for the next eighteen years. Once in charge of the Presidio, Goycoechea went to work at erecting permanent adobe, stone, and tile buildings. He started by building three warehouses for the storage of supplies, a guard house, and barracks for the soldiers.[19]

---

[18] *Ibid.*, pp. 1-4.

[19] Walter A. Tompkins, *Old Spanish Santa Barbara: From Cabrillo to Fremont* (Santa Barbara: McNally and Loftin, 1967), p. 10.

SANTA BARBARA

In August 1790, Goycoechea prepared a census of the Santa Barbara Presidio. According to this census, the total population of the presidio was 230. Of these, 132 were men and 98 were women. Sixty-one men served the presidio as soldiers. The ethnic composition of the presidio inhabitants was as follows: 124 Spaniards (Creoles of unmixed Spanish descent); 52 mestizos (Spanish and Indian mixture), 35 mulattos (Spanish and African descent); 17 Christian Indians from Mexico; four coyotes (so-called from the peculiar coffee-color complexion of their skin), one lobo (Indian and African mixtures), and four of mixed mestizo and mulatto blood. Ten individuals were not classified at all.[20]

When the Santa Barbara Mission was finally founded on December 4, 1786, Father Fermin Fransicso Lasuén presided over the dedication ceremonies. On December 8, 1787, the Mission La Purísima Concepción was founded half-way between Mission Santa Barbara and Mission San Luis Obispo (which had been founded in 1772). Las Purísima Concepción was the eleventh mission built along the *El Camino Real* in Alta California. By this time, the Presidio of Santa Barbara was charged with protection of four missions: San Luis Obispo, San Buenaventura, Santa Barbara, and Purísima Concepción.

---

[20] *Provincial State Papers*, Benicia, Military, XIII, pp. 448-454.

SANTA BARBARA

For almost two decades, the Santa Barbara Presidio was the home for several families of my ancestors. The lives of these ancestors will be discussed in the following chapters.

THE RELUCTANT SETTLER

> *The first families of Los Angeles who had arrived with Governor Neve were as follows: two native Spaniards married to Indian wives; one mestizo, two Negroes, two mulattoes and four Indians, all with Mulatto Indian wves; twenty-two children, some of whom were born on the long journey from Sonora, Sinaloa, and Baja, making a total of forty-four. They received the same pay and rations as the Spanish soldiers... These pioneers were the nucleus of what was to become one of the largest and most advanced cities in the world.*[1]

Luis Quintero

Luis Quintero and his wife María Petra Rubio represent one of the eleven original couples to settle with their families at *El Pueblo de Los Angeles* in 1781. They are also my great-great-great-great-great-great-great-grandparents (also referred to as eighth-generation grandparents).

There is some dispute about the origins of Luis Quintero. Luis Quintero was born sometime around 1725. According to his death record, he was born in Guadalajara, Jalisco. But some researchers believe that he may actually have been born in Álamos, the town in which he raised his family and from which he departed in the Expedition of 1781. And some historians believe that he was the

---

[1] Roy Elmer Whitehead, M.D., *Lugo: A Chronicle of Early California* (Redlands, California: San Bernardino County Museum Association, 1978), p. 87.

THE RELUCTANT SETTLER

son of a black slave and an Indian woman.[2] Luis' wife, María Petra Rubio, was born in 1741 at Álamos, Sonora. It is believed that they were married in Álamos around 1760. Although the baptism and marriage records for the Catholic Church in Álamos extend back to the Seventeenth Century, there are numerous gaps in the documentary record. This lack of continuity prevents us from having a clear understanding of my Quintero and Rubio ancestors.

The surname *Quintero* is said to be derived from *quinto* (one-fifth). Quinto refers to the tenant who delivers one-fifth of his crop to the landlord. The surname *Rubio* is believed to refer to one with red hair or a ruddy complexion. Derived from the Latin *robeus*, referring to the color of ruby, in earlier centuries it may have referred to one who had a light complexion or came from Rubio in Spain.[3]

When Captain Rivera assembled his crew of soldiers and settlers in Álamos in January of 1781, Luis Quintero's destiny was already tied to the historic expedition about to take place. On January 21,

---

[2]Antonio Rios-Bustamante, *Mexican Los Angeles*, p. 44.

[3]Richard D. Woods and Grace Alvarez-Altman, *Spanish Surnames in the Southwestern United States: A Dictionary* (Boston, Massachusetts: G. K. Hall & Co., 1978), pp. 113-114, 121-122.

THE RELUCTANT SETTLER

his 16-year-old daughter Catharina was married at Purísima Concepción Church in Álamos to one of Rivera's soldiers, Joaquin Rodríquez. His 15-year-old daughter, Fabiana Sebastiana, was married to another soldier of the expedition, Eugenio Valdés, on the same day. And, on the following day, Luis's eldest daughter, 18-year-old María Juana Josefa, was united in marriage with still another *soldado de cuera*, José Rosalino Fernández. On the following page, we shall present a Descendancy Chart indicating the twelve generations from Luis Quintero to my two children, Ryan and Jessica Vo.

The prospect of never seeing his daughters again may have played a role in the decision-making process, for it is believed that Luis Quintero was the last *poblador* to sign on the dotted line. When the settlers left Álamos on February 2, 1781, Luis, María Petra, and their eight children were among them. In addition to the three married daughters, María Concepcíon (9 years old), María Tomasa (7), María Rafaela (6), and José Clemente (3) made the 950-mile journey. Sixteen-year-old María Gertrudis Castelo came along as an adopted daughter.[4] On August 18, 1781, Luis Quintero and the other *pobladores* arrived at the San Gabriel Mission after a journey of six-and-a-half months.

---

[4]Thomas Workman Temple II, "Soldiers and Settlers of the Expedition of 1781," *op. cit.*, pp. 103-104.

THE RELUCTANT SETTLER

1. **Luis Quintero (b.1725-Guadalajara;d.1810)**
   sp: Maria Petra Rubio (b.1741-Alamos,Sonora;d.1802)
   └ 2. Maria Josefa Quintero (b.1763-Alamos,Sonora)
       sp: Jose Rosalino Fernandez (b.1756-El Fuerte,Sinaloa;m.1781)
       └ 3. Maria Luciana Fernandez (b.1782-San Gabriel,CA;d.1838)
           sp: Jose Pablo Olivas (b.1780-Rosario,Sinaloa;m.1800;d.1817)
           └ 4. Jose Dolores Olivas (b.1802-Santa Barbara,CA)
               sp: Maria Gertrudis Valenzuela (b.1813-San Gabriel,CA;m.1829)
               └ 5. Maria Antonia Olivas (b.1834-Santa Barbara,CA;d.1908)
                   sp: Apolinario Esquivel (b.1805-Irapuato,Mexico;m.1849;d.1886)
                   └ 6. Regina Esquivel (b.1851-Santa Barbara,CA;d.1891)
                       sp: Gregorio Ortega (b.1825-Mexico;m.1870;d.1916)
                       └ 7. Valentine Ortega (b.1875-Santa Paula,CA;d.1918)
                           sp: Theodora Tapia (b.1876-Los Angeles,CA;m.1893)
                           └ 8. Isabel Ortega (b.1902-Saticoy,CA;d.1979)
                               sp: Refugio Melendez (b.1893-Penjamo,Guanajuato;d.1964)
                               └ 9. Theodora Melendez (b.1927-Saticoy,CA)
                                   sp: Eusebio Basulto (b.1927-Ocotlan,Jalisco)
                                   └ 10. Sarah Paz Basulto (b.1949-Sylmar,CA)
                                       sp: David Charles Kunkel (b.1949-Grand Prairie,TX)
                                       └ 11. Jennifer C. Kunkel (b.1968-Sylmar,CA)
                                           sp: James Dung Vo (b.1968-Saigon,Vietnam;m.1993)
                                           ├ 12. Ryan James Vo (b.1995-Mission Hills,CA)
                                           └ 12. Jessica Saramai Vo (b.1998-Granada Hills,CA)

Descendancy Chart from Luis Quintero

THE RELUCTANT SETTLER

On September 4, 1781, when the pueblo of Los Angeles was first dedicated, Luis Quintero was tallied as a 55-year-old Negro. His wife, María Petra Rubio, was classified as a 40-year-old mulata. Very little is known about Luis Quintero's activities in the first half year at the pueblo. But, on March 22 and 25, 1782, Luis served as *padrino* (God-father) for the Indians confirmed by Father Serra at the San Gabriel Mission. However, a day later, on March 26, 1782, Luis and two other settlers were expelled from Los Angeles by order of Governor de Neve and "sent away as useless to the pueblo and themselves." Their properties confiscated by the authorities, Luis and his family joined the Santa Barbara Company on their journey to the northwest.

In analyzing the causes of Luis Quintero's expulsion from Los Angeles in 1782, it should be noted that the tailor Luis Quintero was probably not well suited for the rigors of frontier life. He was not a farmer and, at the age of 55, it was not likely that he could have adjusted effortlessly to the profession of farmer. It should also be noted that three of Luis' daughters had married soldiers who were attached to the Expedition of 1781. All three of these soldiers (José Rosalino Fernández, Joaquin Rodríguez, and Eugenio Valdés) were destined to be stationed at the Santa Barbara Presidio in the Spring of 1782, and it is possible that the Quintero family hoped to be closer to those daughters. Whatever

THE RELUCTANT SETTLER

the case may be, it is known that Luis Quintero lived out the remaining 28 years of his life as a respectable member of the budding Santa Barbara community.

In the years following his departure from Los Angeles, Luis Quintero worked as a *maestro sastre* (master tailor) for the soldiers at the presidio.[5] In the December 31, 1785 census of the Real Presidio de Santa Barbara, Luis Quintero was listed as a 62-year-old mulato. His wife, M. Petra, was listed as a 45-year-old mulata. They had one child living with them (a son).[6] In the Santa Barbara census of 1790, Luis Quintero was listed as a 65-year-old tailor from Guadalajara. His wife, Petra Rubio, was 48 years old. Their son, José Clemente, aged 13, still lived with them.[7]

María Petra Rubio died on November 3, 1802 at the approximate age of 61. Luis Quintero died eight years later on January 17, 1810 and was buried at the Mission. By the time of his death, Luis

---

[5] Evelyn Martinez y Romero, *My Family Back Bone: A Genealogy of Romero, Olivas, Cota, Pico, Eddy, & Story Families* (San Jose, CA: Foothill Printers and Capitol Printing, 1984), p. 65.

[6] *Provincial State Papers, Missions*, I, 5-10.

[7] "Las Familias de California," *Southern California Quarterly* Vol. XLII, No. 1 (March 1960), pp. 90-92; Provincial State Papers, Benicia Military, XIII, 448-454; State Papers, Missions, I, 96

had watched as the Santa Barbara Presidio expanded beyond the confines of the presidio walls. During the time of his residence (from 1782 to 1810), Luis saw the population of Santa Barbara increase from 150 to 370. This number represented 19 percent of the total California Hispanic population of 1,926 in 1810.[8]

Although Luis Quintero never returned to Los Angeles, many of his descendants did make their home in the small pueblo. His daughter, Sebastiana Quintero and her husband Eugenio Valdés, had nine children between 1782 and 1799, during which time, Eugenio had served at the Santa Barbara Presidio and in the *escolta* at San Buenaventura. After Eugenio retired from the military in 1800, he moved with his wife and family to Los Angeles where he was given lands, which he cultivated until his death.[9] The couple had one more child in 1801 and were registered in the 1804 census at Los Angeles with three of their children: Antonio María, Basilio, and María.[10]

---

[8]Carolyn Gale McGovern, *op. cit.*, p. 154.

[9]Maynard Geiger, "Six Census Records of Los Angeles and Its Immediate Area Between 1804 and 1823," *Southern California Quarterly*, Vol. LIV, No. 4 (Winter 1972), p. 324.

[10]*Ibid.*, p. 316.

THE RELUCTANT SETTLER

Eugenio and Sebastiana's fifth child, María Rita Quiteria Valdés, was married on February 16, 1808 in Los Angeles to a soldier named Vicente Ferrer Villa. This graunddaughter of Luis Quintero was eventually widowed with a large family to support. In 1852, María Rita Valdés de Villa petitioned for confirmation of patent granted in 1838 for the 4,539-acre ranch, Rodeo de las Aguas (Meeting of the Waters). The house María built stood near the present corner of Sunset Boulevard and Alpine Drive. In 1854, María Rita decided to sell Rancho de las Aguas for about $4,000 to Major Henry Hancock, a New Hampshire attorney, and Benjamin Wilson, a native of Nashville, Tennessee. This property eventually became what we now call Beverly Hills.

THE CALIFORNIA SOLDIERS

Who am I – the one whose gaze
Falls searching to the West
And lights upon the coral Sands of Time;
Falling, steady, on this heaving breast,
Co-mingling waves of other place and clime?

I'm a Mexican 'Soldado'
With wild stories to tell –
I am a rugged Pioneer beneath a Mission Bell,
And as the ceaseless ebb and flow
Of ever changing tide
Create strange, new sensations deep inside,
Releasing inhibitions – soft I twirl,
And find myself a South Sea Island Girl.

I am not now – nor can I ever be
Just one of them – for I am all of them,
And they of me.
Who am I? – I am Everyone
Of all my Forebears pasts –
A Captain, Rancher, Chamberlain,
A Minister, A King,
A Pioneer, a Scholar, a Seaman – Everything!

I am what courses through my veins
From Sea – to Sea – to Sea __
I am my Antecedents –
And they are one in me![1]

Pedro Gabriel Valenzuela

On May 12, 1752, the young couple Clemente de Balenzuela (Valenzuela) and Manuela Mendes brought their newborn son to

---

[1] Barbara Juarez Wilson, *From Mission to Majesty: A Genealogy and History of Early California and Royal European Ancestors* (Baltimore, Maryland: Gateway Press, Inc., 1983), p. ii.

THE CALIFORNIA SOLDIERS

Purísima Concepción Church in Álamos, Sonora. In accordance with Roman Catholic doctrine, Father Pedro Gabriel de Aragon baptized the infant child, giving him the Christian name, Pedro Gabriel. As soon as the ceremony ended, the young couple left the church with their small child, while Father Pedro attended to the next couple who had come for another baptism.

Once the second ceremony was finished, Father Pedro went to his small church office and opened the church's Baptismal book. Taking pen in hand, he recorded the baptism of his namesake, listing both the parents and the child's godmother, Ana María de Aragon, as witnesses to the ceremony. With this event 251 years ago, the documented history of my family begins. Clemente de Balenzuela and his young wife represent one set of my eighth-generation grandparents, and their son, Pedro Gabriel, would become one of California's earliest soldier pioneers. My descent from these individuals is presented in the Descendancy Chart on the following page.

Six years later, another significant event would take place at Purísima Concepción. On November 30, 1760, Father Pedro administered the sacrament of Holy Matrimony to Francisco Xavier Parra and María Gabriela de la Vega. Francisco was the son of Nicolas Alberto Parra and Bernarda Miranda, while María

THE CALIFORNIA SOLDIERS

1. Clemente Balenzuela
  sp: Manuela Mendes
└ 2. Pedro Gabriel Valenzuela (b.1752-Alamos,Sonora;d.1826)
   sp: Maria Dolores Parra (b.1763-Alamos,Sonora;m.1781;d.1811)
   └ 3. Antonio Maria Valenzuela (b.1788-Santa Barbara,CA;d.1841)
    sp: Maria Antonia Feliz (b.1788-Santa Barbara,CA;m.1807)
    └ 4. Maria Gertrudis Valenzuela (b.1813-San Gabriel,CA)
     sp: Jose Dolores Olivas (b.1802-Santa Barbara,CA;m.1829)
     └ 5. Maria Antonia Olivas (b.1834-Santa Barbara,CA;d.1908)
      sp: Apolinario Esquivel (b.1805-Irapuato,Mexico;m.1849;d.1886)
      └ 6. Regina Esquivel (b.1851-Santa Barbara,CA;d.1891)
       sp: Gregorio Ortega (b.1825-Mexico;m.1870;d.1916)
       └ 7. Valentine Ortega (b.1875-Santa Paula,CA;d.1918)
        sp: Theodora Tapia (b.1876-Los Angeles,CA;m.1893)
        └ 8. Isabel Ortega (b.1902-Saticoy,CA;d.1979)
         sp: Refugio Melendez (b.1893-Penjamo,Guanajuato;d.1964)
         └ 9. Theodora Melendez (b.1927-Saticoy,CA)
          sp: Eusebio Basulto (b.1927-Ocotlan,Jalisco)
          └ 10. Sarah Paz Basulto (b.1949-Sylmar,CA)
           sp: David Charles Kunkel (b.1949-Grand Prairie,TX)
           └ 11. Jennifer C. Kunkel (b.1968-Sylmar,CA)
            sp: James Dung Vo (b.1968-Saigon,Vietnam;m.1993)
            ├ 12. Ryan James Vo (b.1995-Mission Hills,CA)
            └ 12. Jessica Saramai Vo (b.1998-Granada Hills,CA)

Descendancy Chart from Clemente Balenzuela

THE CALIFORNIA SOLDIERS

Gabriela de la Vega was the daughter of Manuel and María Margareta Vega. Both sets of parents have equal status as my ninth-generation grandparents. Three years later, on September 21, 1763, Francisco Parra and Gabriela de la Vega brought their second-born child to Purísima Concepción to be baptized. This daughter, María Dolores Thomasa Parra, would one day become the wife of her fellow villager, Pedro Gabriel Valenzuela.

It is believed that Pedro Gabriel Valenzuela enlisted in the 1770s as a soldado de cuera. In 1780, when Captain Rivera searched through Sinaloa and Sonora for recruits for El Nuevo Establecimiento de Monterey ("The New Establishment of Monterey"), Pedro signed up. Rivera had instructions to encourage the soldiers to marry before embarking on their journey to Alta California. So it was that on January 29, 1781, the church documents at Purísima Concepción Church tell us that the 30-year-old soldier, Pedro Valenzuela, married 15-year-old Dolores Parra. While Pedro was listed as a mestizo and Dolores was classified as a mulata, they both stated that they were natives of Álamos.

Three months later, Pedro and María Dolores departed from Álamos. All the soldiers and settlers who took part in this expedition to Alta California, although illiterate, were well aware of the great risks along the way, as well as the hardships they faced once they reached their destination. The Apache depredations along the Sonora frontier in recent decades had struck terror into the hearts of prospective settlers and soldiers. The massacre of Captain Rivera and other soldiers and settlers on July 18 would only heighten these fears. On July 14, 1781, Pedro Gabriel Valenzuela and María Dolores Parra arrived at the San Gabriel Mission. Although they were childless at the time of their arrival at San Gabriel, Pedro and María Dolores would eventually have a total of twelve children.[2]

On October 4, 1781, Pedro Valenzuela was listed as one of the soldiers who was stationed at the San Gabriel Mission. Because more experienced presidial soldiers were brought to San Gabriel for the proposed construction of the Santa Barbara Presidio, Pedro was required to replace one of those soldiers taken from the San Diego Presidio. A list of soldiers compiled by Lieutenant José de Zúñiga, the commander of the San Diego Presidio, listed Pedro Valenzuela among the fifty-two men stationed at the San Diego Presidio on May 20, 1782. Pedro was classified as a 24-year-old mestizo from Alamos. He was also listed as illiterate and recently

---

[2]Thomas Workman Temple II, "Soldiers and Settlers of the Expedition of 1781," *op. cit.*, pp. 114-115.

married.³ In fact, Pedro was closer to 31 years of age and it is believed that his illiteracy may have prompted him to give his age incorrectly. Pedro Valenzuela remained at San Diego at least through 1783, after which, it is believed he was dispatched with his small family to the Santa Barbara Presidio. Pedro Valenzuela was listed as a soldier at the Santa Barbara garrison on November 3, 1787.⁴

On August 21, 1790, Captain Goycoechea submitted a report to Governor Fages listing the names of the soldiers and residents of Real Presidio de Santa Barbara. This census reported that sixty-one officers and soldiers were serving at the Presidio. Along with six other men (including Luis Quintero), and the wives and children of the soldiers, the total number of people living in the presidio was 230.⁵

---

³Bill Mason, "The Garrisons of San Diego Presidio, 1770-1794," *The Journal of San Diego History*, Fall 1978 (Vol. XXIV, No. 4), pp. 412-413.

⁴ State Papers, Sacramento, I, 5-8.

⁵ Provincial State Papers, Benicia Military, XIII, 448-454; State Papers, Missions, I, 96; "Las Familias de California," *op. cit.*, pp. 90-92.

THE CALIFORNIA SOLDIERS

In the 1790 census, Pedro Valenzuela was listed as a 36-year-old Spaniard (criollo) and a native of Sinaloa. His wife María Dolores Parra was a 29-year-old mestiza. Also listed were their three children: José María, (8 years old); José Antonio, (4); and Antonio María (six months of age).

The life of the California presidial soldier involved a wide range of duties, many of which did not seem to fit into a military description. While they occasionally went on expeditions to other presidios or tracked down horse thieves, a great deal of their time, according to Leon G. Campbell, "was devoted to escorting priests to and from the missions, caring for the king's herds, and tilling the soil."[6]

According to early census records from the Pueblo of Los Angeles, Pedro Valenzuela retired from the military and moved with his wife Dolores to Los Angeles in 1798.[7] However, their family continued to grow and on January 31, their son Vicente Antonio Valenzuela was baptized at the San Gabriel Mission. In

---

[6] Leon G. Campbell, "The First Californios: Presidial Society in Spanish California, 1769-1822," *op. cit.*, p. 590. Copyright © by *Journal of the West, Inc.*, Reprinted with permission of *Journal of the West*, 1531 Yuma, Manhattan, KS 66502, USA.

[7] Maynard Geiger, *op. cit.*, p. 323.

THE CALIFORNIA SOLDIERS

1804, Pedro and Dolores were listed, along with two of their children, Antonio and María Antonia, as residents of Los Angeles.[8] Two years later, on February 27, 1806, the last of their twelve children, José Antonio, would be baptized at San Gabriel Mission.

On April 11, 1811, María Dolores Parra died at the Pueblo of Los Angeles and was buried at the San Gabriel Mission.[9] In 1823, the widower Pedro Valenzuela was listed as a resident of Los Angeles, along with two of his children, Estanislao and J. Antonio.[10] When Pedro Gabriel Valenzuela died on April 3, 1827 at the age of 68, he was buried at the San Gabriel Mission.[11]

Juan Matias Olivas

Juan Matias Olivas was born in 1758 near Rosario, Sinaloa, as the son of Francisco Olivas and María Goralsa. On May 25, 1777, at about 19 years of age, Juan Matias was married at Nuestra Señora del Rosario Church to María Dorotea Espinosa.

---

[8]*Ibid.*, p. 316.

[9]San Gabriel Mission Death Records, Number 3073.

[10]Maynard Geiger, *op. cit.*, pp. 334-341.

[11]San Gabriel Mission Death Records, Number 5124.

THE CALIFORNIA SOLDIERS

The life of Juan Matias seemed uneventful until August 6, 1780, when he volunteered to become a soldier of the Establecimiento de Monterey ("The Establishment of Monterey"). Juan's military record gives us an idea of how he looked. He was described as being 5 feet, 2 inches tall, Catholic, with black eyes, black hair, and olive skin. He was described as having sharp features and several scars on his face.[12]

Most interesting to me is that at a time when most men wore beards, Juan Matias Olivas is described as clean-shaven. Because he was of predominantly Indian blood, he may have been unable to grow a beard at all.

In November 1780, when Captain Rivera came to Rosario seeking recruits for his planned expedition to Alta California, Juan Matias signed up. Along with his wife, María Dorothea Espinosa, then 23 years old, and their two infant children, María Nicolasa and José Pablo, Juan Matias traveled to Álamos where all the soldiers and settlers were to be assembled. From here, Juan Matias and his family were assigned to accompany the settlers on their journey north.[13]

---

[12] Simancas, Secretaría de Guerra, Legajo 7029, Expediente 1, páginas 126-136.

[13] Thomas Workman Temple II, "Soldiers and Settlers of the Expedition of 1781,"

THE CALIFORNIA SOLDIERS

In the months following their arrival at the San Gabriel Mission on August 18, 1781, Juan Matias Olivas and his family were housed near the mission. While Juan Matias attended to his soldierly duties, young María Dorotea cared for their infant children. When the Santa Barbara Presidio was founded on April 21, 1782, Juan Matias was there. Juan and María Dorotea's third child, Juan de Dios de la Luz, was born during the next year and was the eighth child to be baptized at Santa Barbara on March 28, 1783.

A look at the July 1, 1784 "Disbursement of Presidio," as compiled by Captain Goycoechea, provides us with a good example of the many duties of presidial soldiers. The summary showed the activities of the sixty officers and men who were stationed at the presidio on that day:[14]

On guard in the presidio	10
Guarding the horses	5
On duty in San Buenaventura	15
Watchman for the town of Los Angeles	1
On the frontier of the Californias	1
With the mail service to San Diego	4
Cutting timber in Monterey	1

---

op. cit., p. 105.
[14] *Archivo General de la Nación, Obras Públicas,* tomo 15.

THE CALIFORNIA SOLDIERS

With the mule train to the town of Los Angeles (including Juan Matias)	5
Available for duty	18
Total	60

It is interesting to note the contrasts between the 1784 manpower disbursement and the Goycoechea's December 31, 1788 report for the garrison:[15]

On guard in the presidio	5
Guarding the horses	4
On duty in San Buenaventura	11
With the mail service to Monterey	3
On duty at Santa Barbara	3
On duty at Purísima Mission	15
On duty at San Gabriel Mission	1
On duty at Loreto Presidio	1
Available for duty	13
Total	59

In describing the lighter side of presidial life, the California historian Charles Chapman wrote that "Life was one continuous round of hospitality and social amenities, tempered with vigorous outdoor sport... Music, games, dancing and sprightly conversation – these were the occupations of the time – these constituted education..." According to Chapman, both men and women "were expert horsemen, could throw a lasso, and shoot unerringly."[16]

---

[15] Provincial State Papers, VII, 273.

[16] Charles Chapman, *op. cit.*, p. 390.

THE CALIFORNIA SOLDIERS

In the first complete census taken at the Real Presidio de Santa Barbara on December 31, 1785, Juan Matias was listed as a 26-year-old mestizo. The census listed his wife, M. Dorotea Olivas, as a 27-year-old mestiza. They had three children.[17] On September 9, 1789 Juan Matias' wife, Dorotea, died, leaving poor Juan Matias a widower with six children: Nicolasa, Pablo, Cosme, Juana, José Delores and Madeline.[18] On the following page is a Descendancy Chart illustrating my family's descent from Francisco Olivas to the present day.

Not long after he was widowed, Juan Matias Olivas was tallied in the 1790 census of the Real Presidio de Santa Barbara.[19] Listed as a 31-year-old widower, Juan was classified was an Indian and a native of Rosario. Four of his six children were listed with their respective ages: María Nicolasa (11 ½); Juan Pablo (9 ½); Cosme (6); and María de Los Santos (2). By now, the entire population of the Santa Barbara Presidio had reached 230 individuals,

---

[17] State Papers, Missions, I, 5-10.

[18] Death Register, Santa Barbara Presidio, No. 14 (Sept. 9, 1789).

[19] Provincial State Papers, Benicia Military, XIII, 448-454; State Papers, Missions, I, 96; "Las Familias de California," *op. cit.*, pp. 90-92.

THE CALIFORNIA SOLDIERS

1. Francisco Olivas
  sp: Maria Goralsa
  └ 2. Juan Matias Olivas (b.1759-Rosario,Sinaloa;d.1806)
      sp: Maria Dorotea Espinosa (b.1758-Rosario,Sinaloa;m.1777;d.1806)
      └ 3. Jose Pablo Olivas (b.1780-Rosario,Sinaloa;d.1817)
          sp: Maria Luciana Fernandez (b.1782-San Gabriel,CA;m.1800;d.1838)
          └ 4. Jose Dolores Olivas (b.1802-Santa Barbara,CA)
              sp: Maria Gertrudis Valenzuela (b.1813-San Gabriel,CA;m.1829)
              └ 5. Maria Antonia Olivas (b.1834-Santa Barbara,CA;d.1908)
                  sp: Apolinario Esquivel (b.1805-Irapuato,Mexico;m.1849;d.1886)
                  └ 6. Regina Esquivel (b.1851-Santa Barbara,CA;d.1891)
                      sp: Gregorio Ortega (b.1825-Mexico;m.1870;d.1916)
                      └ 7. Valentine Ortega (b.1875-Santa Paula,CA;d.1918)
                          sp: Theodora Tapia (b.1876-Los Angeles,CA;m.1893)
                          └ 8. Isabel Ortega (b.1902-Saticoy,CA;d.1979)
                              sp: Refugio Melendez (b.1893-Penjamo,Guanajuato;d.1964)
                              └ 9. Theodora Melendez (b.1927-Saticoy,CA)
                                  sp: Eusebio Basulto (b.1927-Ocotlan,Jalisco)
                                  └ 10. Sarah Paz Basulto (b.1949-Sylmar,CA)
                                      sp: David Charles Kunkel (b.1949-Grand Prairie,TX)
                                      └ 11. Jennifer C. Kunkel (b.1968-Sylmar,CA)
                                          sp: James Dung Vo (b.1968-Saigon,Vietnam;m.1993)
                                          ├ 12. Ryan James Vo (b.1995-Mission Hills,CA)
                                          └ 12. Jessica Saramai Vo (b.1998-Granada Hills,CA)

Descendancy Chart from Francisco Olivas

THE CALIFORNIA SOLDIERS

comprising 24 percent of the entire Hispanic population of Alta California.[20]

On November 10, 1793, the English Captain George Vancouver, with a fleet of three ships, sailed into Santa Barbara's harbor. Goycoechea welcomed his English visitors with open arms and gave them a tour of the presidio. During this eight-day visit at Santa Barbara, Vancouver was received with "the greatest earnestness and cordiality." Upon leaving, Vancouver wrote that the presidio "excelled in neatness, cleanliness, and other smaller, though essential comforts."[21]

In March 1794, Spain declared war against France. Eventually the news of this war arrived in California. The soldiers became acutely aware of the fact that both France and England yearned for the opportunity to take California into their own empires. But it was not likely that the two hundred and seventy-five soldiers at the four presidios in California could have held off a serious invasion by a foreign power. Nevertheless, the presidio was their home and steps were taken to safeguard the safety of their families and possessions in case of attack.

---

[20]Carolyn Gale McGovern, *op. cit.*, p. 154.

[21]George Vancouver, *A Voyage of Discovery to the North Pacific Ocean* (London, 1798).

THE CALIFORNIA SOLDIERS

On June 1, 1794, Juan Matias married Juana de Dios Ontiveros at the San Gabriel Mission. After their marriage, Matias and Juana had a son named José Herculano. Two years later, another son, Lazaro, was born, but lived only four months.

In 1800, Juan Matias Olivas retired from the military and – with his wife and younger children – took up residence in the small pueblo of Los Angeles. By this time, the small pueblo had seventy families, 315 people, and consisted of 30 small adobe houses. In 1804, Juan Olivas was listed in the Los Angeles census as a retired soldier. Living with him were his wife, Juana Ontiveros, and their children: Cosme, María, and Juana Olivas, and Pedro Ontiveros. Juan was given lands which he was cultivated until his death in 1806.[22]

José Rosalino Fernández

José Rosalino Fernández was born in 1761 in Villa del Fuerte, Sinaloa, as the son of Miguel Fernández and María Quiteria Feliz. It is believed that José Rosalino, Eugenio Valdés, and one other soldier enlisted with Rivera's expedition in the middle of 1780 when Rivera came through El Fuerte looking for soldiers willing to accompany his expedition to Alta California. As noted above, it

---

[22]Maynard Geiger, *op. cit.*, pp. 316, 322-324.

THE CALIFORNIA SOLDIERS

was strongly recommended by the authorities that the soldiers on the expedition be married men. For that reason a flurry of marriages involving soldiers took place at Purísima Concepción Church in Álamos in the months before the expedition's departure.

On January 22, 1781, Eugenio Valdés, a native of El Fuerte and son of Roque Valdés and Manuela Fernandez was married to Sebastiana Quintero, the daughter of the expedition's tailor, Luis Quintero. José Rosalino, who may have been his cousin, was one of the witnesses to the wedding. Shortly after, a second wedding took place between the 30-year-old mestizo, José Rosalino Fernández and the 21-year-old mulata, Juana Josefa Quintero. Juana Josefa, another daughter of Luis Quintero, stated that she was a native of Álamos. Eugenio Valdés served as a witness at this wedding.

Three months later, José Rosalino Fernández and María Josefa Quintero left with Rivera on the journey north. In July, the expedition reached the junction of the Gila and Colorado Rivers, where most of the soldiers, including José Rosalino Fernandez, Pedro Gabriel Valenzuela, and their families, were sent ahead to San Gabriel. This group arrived safely at the San Gabriel Mission on July 14, 1781.

THE CALIFORNIA SOLDIERS

Not long after, however, word reached San Gabriel about events that took place after the soldiers left Rivera. On the night of July 18th, Rivera and a small contingent of soldiers were massacred by Yuma Indians as they camped on the bank of the Colorado. This slaughter would not be soon forgotten and weighed heavily on the minds of both settlers and soldiers. For the rest of 1781, the soldiers and their families would be stationed at the San Gabriel Mission, pending the establishment of the Santa Barbara Presidio. Their infant daughter María Luciana was baptized on January 8, 1782 at Mission San Gabriel.

Nowhere in California was the density of the Indian population greater than in the Santa Barbara/San Buenaventura coastal region inhabited by the Chumash Indians. Although the initial relations between the Spanish authorities and the Indian chiefs had been good, military policy required that each mission be garrisoned by an *escolta* (escort) of soldiers. Early on, José Rosalino Fernández was one of the soldiers chosen to form part of the escolta at San Buenaventura, twenty-seven miles from the presidio. In the July 1, 1784 roll call of the Santa Barbara Company, Rosalino Fernández was one of the fifteen presidial guards on duty at San Buenaventura.[23]

---

[23] *Archivo General de la Nación, Obras Públicas*, tomo 15.

THE CALIFORNIA SOLDIERS

When Goycoechea conducted the December 31,1785 census of the Real Presidio de Santa Barbara, Rosalino Fernández was listed as a 28-year-old mulato. His family included his wife, M. Juana, a 22-year-old mulata, and their three children. In the Santa Barbara Census of 1790, Rosalino Fernández was classified as a 32-year-old native of Fuerte. His wife, Juana Quintero, was listed as 27 years of age. Their children listed were: María Luciana (9); María Isabel (7); Antonio (5); María Josefa (4); María Felipe (2); and María Marcela (6 months).[24]

It was the support of the soldiers' wives, such as Juana, that made presidial life more tolerable than it may have been without the presence of the spouses. Because José Rosalino was frequently on patrol to San Gabriel, San Buenaventura, or Los Angeles, Juana had to care for the children and tend the small garden plot that the soldiers' families were permitted to keep. It was necessary for the lady of the house to raise the stock until the children were old enough to help with such responsibilities. In addition, María Juana and the other wives were able to sew and make footwear for the soldiers and the children.

---

[24]State Papers, Missions, I, 5-10; "Las Familias de California," *op. cit.*, pp. 90-92.

THE CALIFORNIA SOLDIERS

By the end of 1794, the total population of the presidio – both soldiers and their families – was two hundred eighty-five and growing. On December 31, 1798, Rosalino Fernández was listed as one of 54 soldiers at the Santa Barbara Presidio.[25] But, after this time, we lose track of José Rosalino. It is known, however, that he was in San Blas at the time of María Luciana's marriage in 1800, and it is likely that he died in Nayarit, far to the south of Californian shores.

---

[25]*Provincial State Papers*, Benecia Military, Vol. XVII, p. 20.

THE FELIZ FAMILY

Every mission and presidio had soldiers attached to it, the number depending on the nature of the local Indians... Soldiers used and wore weapons of both offense and defense. They were the only people who used guns and ammunition, having short barreled muskets. Each carried a sword or lance.... Practically every male Spaniard carried a knife on his person, and some of the women did, knives being highly prized weapons.... The soldiers were the policemen of the missions. When the wild Indians stole livestock or property, the soldiers chased them and usually brought them back and imprisoned them, each garrison having a guard house for that purpose.[1]

Anastasio María Feliz

Anastasio María Feliz was born in Álamos around 1749 as the son of Juan Blas Feliz and Ana Geronima de Castro. The surname Feliz is a very famous name in Sonora. Geronimo Feliz, who was born around 1660, was one of the earliest settlers of Sonora. Members of his family had come to Sonora from Sinaloa and settled in the area of Baroyeca, which is in the jurisdiction of Álamos. Feliz family activites centered on both silver mining and ranching, and Geronimo Feliz became a large land-holder in Baroyeca. Geronimo Feliz was married to Isabela Romero. His son, Captain Nicolas Feliz was married to Mara Margarita de Leon.[2]

---

[1] Roy Elmer Whitehead, *op. cit.*, pp. 102-103.

[2] Lillian Ramos Wold, *Hispanic Surnames: History and Genealogy* (Midway City, CA: SHHAR Press, 1994), p. 54.

THE FELIZ FAMILY

Nicolas Feliz and María Margarita de Leon had four known children, including Joseph Feliz (the oldest), who held the title of Capitan de Guerra. He married Manuela Antonia Ezquerr in 1731 and they became the parents of José Vicente Feliz, a cousin to Anastasio María Feliz and the man who would become well-known in Los Angeles as "Little Father of the Pueblo."[3]

In March 1774, Anastasio María Feliz enlisted in the army in Villa de Sinaloa, and soon after went to California.[4] He was first stationed at Tubac (Nogales) and the San Diego Presidio. On January 1, 1780, he was listed in a roll call of the soldiers at the San Diego Presidio.[5] It was a year later that Captain Ortega would bring Anastacio to Santa Barbara to assist in the training of the new recruits there.

On August 28, 1781, Anastasio María Feliz was married to María Gertrudis Valenzuela at the San Gabriel Mission.[6] María Gertrudis, also a native of Álamos, had been born around 1768 as the daughter of Francisco Xavier Valenzuela and María Rita

---

[3] *Ibid.*

[4] Simancas, Secretaría de Guerra, Legajo 7026, Expedience 1.

[5] Bill Mason, *op. cit.*, pp 409-411.

[6] San Gabriel Marriage Book, #140.

THE FELIZ FAMILY

Quijada. Francisco Valenzuela was the son of Santiago Balenzuela and Josepha de Cotta, while Rita Quijada was the daughter of Juan Ataxia Quijada and Rosa Carrio. The two had been married on September 20, 1767 at Purisima Concepcíon Church in Álamos, and soon after, María Gertrudes was born.

María Gertrudis had accompanied her uncle, Vicente Quijada, on the Expedition of 1781 and arrived at San Gabriel on July 14, 1781. Her parents did not join the expedition and stayed in Álamos. The surname Quijada is the name of places in Argentina and Costa Rica. This surname, which means jaws, was one of the original surnames considered by Cervantes for Don Quijote.[7]

While Anastasio Feliz was stationed at Monterey, a military inventory dated April 15, 1782 was distributed to company commanders. This list called for the transfer of Anastacio María Feliz to the Santa Barbara Presidio.[8] On May 28, 1783, Anastacio Feliz and Gertrudis Valenzuela baptized their first-born child, Juan José Anastacio Feliz, at Santa Barbara.

---

[7]Richard D. Woods and Grace Alvarez-Altman, *op. cit.*, p. 113.

[8]*Provincial State Papers*, Benicia Military, II, pp. 13-14.

THE FELIZ FAMILY

In addition to protecting the presidio against a possible Indian attack or foreign invasion, the soldiers had many duties: "to explore the interior country, catch horse thieves, care for the animals and fields of the King, create their own food supplies and carry the mail."[9] According to a rollcall of the soldiers at the Royal Presidio of Santa Barbara on July 1, 1784, Anastasio Feliz was on duty at San Buenaventura Mission, along with Rosalino Fernández and thirteen other Santa Barbara soldiers.[10]

The Governor also had concerns for the safety of the people at the pueblo. As a result of these concerns, a contingent of four soldiers under the command of José Vicente Feliz was sent to stay at the Los Angeles Pueblo in 1787 to safeguard its development and well-being.[11] Vicente Feliz was, as a matter of fact, the cousin of my ancestor, Anastacio Feliz who had already been stationed for a few years in California.

In the December 31, 1785 census of the Real Presidio de Santa Barbara, Anastacio Feliz was classified as a 39 years old and of

---

[9] Barbara Schneidau, *A Guide to Old Santa Barbara: The Spanish and Mexican Periods* (Santa Barbara, 1977), pp. 6-7.

[10] *Archivo General de la Nación, Obras Públicas,* tomo 15.

[11] W.W. Robinson, op. cit., p. 13.

THE FELIZ FAMILY

Spanish descent. His 17-year-old wife, María Gertrudes was also listed as Spanish.[12] In the 1790 census of the Real Presidio de Santa Barbara, Anastasio María Feliz was listed as a 45-year-old native of Los Álamos. His wife, Gertrudes Valenzuela was 22 years of age, and their three children were listed as follows: Juan José, (8 years old); Ana Geronima (4); and María Antonia (2).[13]

As soldiers at the presidio grew old and retired from the military service, they were permitted to build adobe homes in the Plaza de Invalidos outside of the presidio grounds. These residences would eventually form the nucleus of the town of Santa Barbara, and it is assumed that Anastasio Feliz was among the retirees who stayed close to quarters in the last years of the Eighteenth Century.

On December 31, 1798, Anastasio Feliz was listed as an invalid soldier of the Santa Barbara Presidio.[14] After the turn of the century, however, Anastasio and his family moved to the Rancho Los Feliz owned by his cousin, José Vicente Feliz. In 1804,

---

[12] *Provincial State Papers*, VI, 322-323.

[13] *Provincial State Papers*, Benicia Military, XIII, 448-454; State Papers, Missions, I, 96; "Las Familias de California," *op. cit.*, pp. 90-92.

[14] *Provincial State Papers*, Benecia Military, Vol. XVII, p. 21.

THE FELIZ FAMILY

Anastacio Feliz and his wife Gertrudis Valenzuela were listed as residents of the Los Angeles area, along with their son Juan.[15]

The Rancho Los Feliz was made up of 6,677 acres, granted by Governor Pedro Fages to José Vicente Feliz for his service to the pueblo of Los Angeles. Anastasio María Feliz died at Rancho Los Feliz and was buried at San Gabriel on May 10, 1810. Gertrudis Valenzuela died six years later.

---

[15]Maynard Geiger, *op. cit.*, pp. 316, 319.

FROM SPANISH TO MEXICAN

California can boast of one of the most productive economies the world has ever seen: The Golden State annually produces more goods and services than all but a handful of the world's nations. But during the Spanish colonial period (1769-1821) and the Mexican national period (1822-1846), contemporaries lamented the lack of economic growth in Alta California....

While contemporaries were right to marvel at the rapid expansion of the California economy during and after the Gold Rush, they underestimated the economy of California during the Spanish and Mexican periods. Before 1848, as recent scholarship has shown, Indians, Franciscans, soldiers, settlers, and traders engaged in modes of exchange and production that reflected local and national strategies of economic development. Furthermore, the development during the Spanish and Mexican periods of intensive agriculture, cattle ranching, artisan crafts, and foreign commerce transformed the landscape of California and its native peoples and introduced forms of labor and production that continued into the American period. Thus, economic activity in Spanish and Mexican California, although limited in scale compared to the boom after 1848, contributed to much of the economic growth in the Golden State during and after the Gold Rush.[1]

José Pablo Olivas

According to the Catholic church records of Rosario, Sinaloa, José Pablo Olivas was born on January 25, 1780 as the legitimate son of Juan Matias Olivas and Dorothea Espinosa. Listed as a mulato in the church's baptism records, José Pablo was baptized on

---

[1] Ramón Gutiérrez and Richard J. Orsi, *Contested Eden: California Before the Gold Rush* (Berkeley: University of California Press, 1998), pp. 111-112.

FROM SPANISH TO MEXICAN

February 20 with Manual Theodoro Cillas and María Paula Cillas as his godparents. José Pablo was the second child of the young couple, Juan Matias and Dorothea.

When Juan Matias and Dorotea embarked upon the Expedition of 1781, their two children, Nicolasa and José Pablo, were still infants. Juan Matias Olivas was one of the 17 soldiers assigned to accompany the settlers on the journey north. After a 950-mile painstaking journey up the Baja Peninsula, they arrived at the San Gabriel Mission on August 18, 1781. Because several of the children – perhaps José Pablo was among them – had just recovered from smallpox, the expedition was quarantined outside of the mission for 17 days.

José Pablo grew up within the walls of the Santa Barbara Presidio. Living at close quarters with fifty other families was no easy chore, but the inhabitants of the garrison were united in their camaraderie as the families of soldiers. As a child, José Pablo attended the same church services as his future wife, María Luciana Fernández, the first-born child of the presidial soldier, José Rosalino Fernández, and his wife, Juana Quintero.

By the year 1800, the entire population of the Santa Barbara Presidio had grown to 370 people, which represented more than 21

FROM SPANISH TO MEXICAN

per cent of the total Hispanic population of the state (1,533).² By 1810, the population of the Santa Barbara Presidio increased to 460.³ At about this time, José Pablo stepped into his father's footsteps and became a soldier of the presidio. In a roster of individuals dated February 17, 1804, Pablo Olivas was listed as one of the fifty-four soldiers on active duty at the Santa Barbara Presidio.

On January 7, 1800, José Pablo Olivas was married at Mission Santa Barbara to María Luciana Fernández. According to the marriage record, José Pablo's father, Juan Matias, was then a resident of the Los Angeles pueblo. María Luciana's father José Rosalino Fernández was listed as a resident of San Blas, while her mother was a resident of the Santa Barbara Presidio.⁴ José Pablo Olivas and María Luciana Fernández had eight children born between 1801 and 1812, including my great-great-great-great-great-grandfather, José Dolores de Jesus, who was baptized Nov. 3, 1802 at the Santa Barbara Mission.

---

²Carolyn Gale McGovern, op. cit., p. 154.

³Hubert Howe Bancroft, History of California (San Francisco, 1884-1890), II, p. 118.

⁴Santa Barbara Marriage Record No. 34.

FROM SPANISH TO MEXICAN

Upheaval

In the early Nineteenth Century, wars of independence broke out in most of Spain's Latin American colonies. Mexico's struggle for independence against Spain began on the night of September 15/16, 1810 when a mild-mannered creole priest, Father Miguel de Hidalgo y Castillo, published his famous outcry against tyranny from his parish in the village of Dolores. His impassioned speech – referred to as Grito de Hidalgo ("Cry of Hidalgo") – set into motion a process that would not end until August 24, 1821 with the signing of the Treaty of Córdova.

Because of numerous wars of liberation going on throughout Latin America, the arrival of Spanish supply ships became sparse and undependable. As the supplies dwindled to a mere trickle, the California presidios became dependent upon the missions for food surpluses and manufactured items. By 1813, the Commandante of Santa Barbara informed the Governor that his soldiers were without shirts and had little food; in addition, the presidio soldiers received no pay for three years, and pensions were suspended.

American ships involved in whaling and seal and sea otter hunting had started appearing off the coast. Occasionally, the ships had to put into shore to repair their boats and get supplies. Although Spanish law forbade trade with all foreign nations, the

FROM SPANISH TO MEXICAN

Californians, already famous for their hospitality, did not deny the sailors fresh food. With increasing frequency during the first decade of the Nineteenth Century, American vessels stopped by hidden inlets to barter for skins and cowhides with badly needed household goods from New England. Some of the mission padres and ranchers decided it was better to take the risk of dealing with outsiders than to go without the supplies they needed.

Pablo Olivas died on December 16, 1817 when his son José Dolores was only fifteen years of age.[5] It was during this period of intense upheaval that Pablo's son, José Dolores Olivas, stepped into his shoes to serve as a third-generation soldado de cuera. Pablo's widow, Luciana Raphaela Fernández, would remarry on March 29, 1821 Her second husband was one Juan María Cordero. On October 10, 1838, María Luciana Fernández died at Mission Santa Barbara.

Independence from Spain

In 1821, after years of revolutionary turmoil in Mexico, Agustin de Iturbide declared Mexico to be independent of Spain and made himself Emperor. The name Nueva Espana was supplanted by that of Mexico. Not until January 1822 did news of Iturbide's

---

[5]Death Register, Santa Barbara Presidio, No. 192.

FROM SPANISH TO MEXICAN

victory reached Alta California. In April, California was notified of Mexico's successful revolt against Spain and the California garrisons lowered the Spanish flag and California became a province of the Empire of Mexico. On April 13, 1822, the soldiers at the Santa Barbara Presidio took their oath of allegiance to the new government in Mexico City. On November 19, 1823, Emperor Iturbide was deposed and the Republic of Mexico was established.

One of the most important effects of independence was the opening of the California coast to foreign trade. Over the years, the California rancheros had accumulated large herds of cattle. According to Meredith Stevens in The House of Olivas, the "hides and tallows were a much sought after commodity by the Europeans and Americans."[6] The cattle needed a minimum of care and multiplied rapidly.

The horse population of California increased so quickly that the excess had to be killed off in order to reserve pasturage for the more profitable cattle. Every rancho had its horses broken to riding and everyone – men, women, and children – became skilled horsemen. Only elderly ladies and infant children traveled in the

---

[6]Meredith Stevens, op. cit., p. 3.

creaking and ponderous wagons called carretas. In time, the Californians became famous throughout North America for their horsemanship.

Antonio María Valenzuela

Antonio María Valenzuela and María Antonia Feliz, each the child of soldiers at the Santa Barbara Presidio, probably grew up together and, through their eventual marriage, would become my great-great-great-great-great-great-grandparents. Antonio was baptized on February 1, 1786 at San Gabriel as the son of Pedro Gabriel Valenzuela and María Dolores Parra. María Antonia Dorotea Feliz was born on June 8, 1788 at Santa Barbara as the daughter of Anastasio Feliz and Gertrudis Valenzuela.[7]

In 1798, when Pedro Gabriel retired from the military and moved his family to the small pueblo of Los Angeles, his 12-year-old son, Antonio María Valenzuela, came along. At about the same time, María Antonia's father, Anastasio Feliz also retired to the Rancho Los Feliz, a couple of miles from the pueblo. Living in the same vicinity and as the children of soldiers, the two were betrothed and married in September 1807 at San Gabriel. The small pueblo of Los Angeles was fast becoming "a center for the recruitment of

---

[7]Santa Barbara Mission, Baptism Record No. 50.

soldiers." In 1805, eighteen men were recruited from the pueblo for the San Diego presidial company.[8] On July 25, 1805, 21-year-old Antonio Valenzuela enlisted in the San Diego Company.

In the 1834 Santa Barbara census, Antonio Valenzuela Parra was listed as a 40-year-old campista (field worker) who had been born at Santa Barbara. His 36-year-old wife, María Feliz Valenzuela, claimed to be a native of San Diego. Two children were living with them: Baltasar (12 years old, born in Santa Barbara) and María Trinidad (11 years old, born in Santa Barbara). And living next door was their daughter, 20-year-old daughter, Gertrudis Valenzuela, who was born in Los Angeles. Gertrudis, by this time, had married Dolores Olivas and had four children, including the twins, María Antonia and Susanna Olivas. Antonio Valenzuela died and was buried on July 4, 1841 at Santa Barbara.[9]

---

[8]Bancroft, *History of California*, Vol. 2, p. 101.

[9]Registered Deaths of Santa Barbara Presidio, #422, July 4, 1841.

THE CHANGING OF THE GUARD

The conquest of California by the United States was probably inevitable, given the unbridled energy of a young nation and an open continent stretching to the Pacific. But the schemes to obtain it were not made in heaven. Rather, they were conspicuously human in motivation and achievement. A lust for land, a quest for independence beyond the frontier, trade and profit, the vision of a nation from sea to sea, fear of foreign deterrence: these stirred the spirits of countless Americans. Official exploring expeditions spied out the land, but independent trappers, traders, farmers, and adventurers were drawn westward as into a mighty vacuum, followed by the U.S. Army and Navy. Manifest destiny heralded the invasion – the American people were destined to subdue the continent. Yet, the United States could not await events; Mexico's hold upon California was uncertain, and England must not snatch it from her weakening grasp. We must be first![1]

A Soldier of the Republic

On November 3, 1802, José Dolores de Jesus Olivas was baptized at the Santa Barbara Mission with Cosme Vanegas and his mother María Bernarda Alvarez as witnesses.[2] Dolores would become the third generation of Olivas men to become a *soldado de cuera*. It was his destiny to see the transition of California as it passed from the hands of the Spanish empire to the newly independent Mexican state. And he would serve as a soldier to both nations.

---

[1] Neal Harlow, *California Conquered: War and Peace on the Pacific, 1846-1850* (Berkeley: University of California Press, 1982), p. xv.

[2] Santa Barbara Mission, Baptism Record #249.

THE CHANGING OF THE GUARD

On December 16, 1817, when José Delores was only 15 years old, his father, José Pablo Olivas, passed away. As Pablo's eldest surviving son, José soon stepped into his father's shoes as a soldier at the Santa Barbara Presidio. By 1820, the population of the presidio had reached 500 (in contrast to a population of 230 in 1790). This figure represented almost 27% of the total presidial population in California (1,856) and 20% of the total Hispanic population in that year (2,498).[3]

On June 14, 1829, José Dolores de Jesus Olivas was married to María Gertrudis Valenzuela at Mission Santa Ynez. Dolores Olivas was listed as a single *soldado de cuera* and a native of the Santa Barbara. His bride, Gertrudis, was listed as the legitimate daughter of José Antonio Valenzuela and María Antonia Feliz.[4] María Gertrudis Valenzuela had been baptized sixteen years earlier on June 7, 1813 at the San Gabriel Mission. Like her husband, she was the daughter of a presidial soldier and had spent most of her early years growing up at the presidio.

As José Dolores and Gertrudis prepared to start their family in 1830, they took their position as members of the growing Santa

---

[3] Carolyn Gale McGovern, *op. cit.*, p. 154.

[4] Marriage Records of Gente de Razón at Santa Ines Mission, Number 386.

THE CHANGING OF THE GUARD

Barbara presidial community which now numbered 604. This population represented over one-third of the entire California presidial population (1,806) and over 17% of the entire Hispanic population of the state (1,664).[5]

The children of José Delores and María Gertrudis, with their approximate dates of baptism at the Santa Barbara or San Luis Obispo missions, are listed as follows: 1) José Antonio Santiago (April 1830); 2) Juana de Dios (March 1832); 3) María Antonia Blanca (February 1834); 4) Susanna Blanca (February 1834); 5) Apolinario Guillermo (September 1836); 6) María Eulalia (November 21, 1839); 7) José Ignacio Antonio Victoriano (circa 1840); 8) Mariana Silveria (June 9, 1841); 9) Carolina Celestina (June 1843); 10) Blas Felipe (February 3, 1846); 11) José de los Santos (April 18, 1848); and 12) Nicolas Amado (September 13, 1850).

In the Santa Barbara census of 1834, Delores was listed as married, 32 years of age and a native of Santa Barbara. His wife, Gertrudis Valenzuela, was 20 years of age, and a native of Los Angeles. Their four children were listed as follows: José María (4 years old), Juana (3), María Antonia and Susana (both four months

---

[5] Carolyn Gale McGovern, *op. cit.*, p. 154.

old). All the children, according to the census, had been born in Santa Barbara. Four months earlier on February 4, 1834, the baptism of the twin sisters, María Antonia Blanca and Susana Blanca, had been recorded at the Santa Barbara Presidio.[6]

After serving out his term of enlistment, Delores Olivas retired from the military and became an agricultural laborer. He and his family continued to live in the vicinity of the presidio. By 1840, the presidial community had now grown to 920 people, some 21% of the entire Hispanic population of the state (4,380).[7]

James K. Polk and California

James Knox Polk (1795-1849) was the eleventh president of the United States (1845-1849). From the beginning of his administration, he had a strategy to snatch California from Mexico's rule. During his first year and a half in office, Polk sought to purchase California outright. However, Polk also hoped to encourage revolution among the Mexican and American Californians in the hope that they would then seek admission to the Union. If the first two steps failed, Polk envisioned the forcible seizure of California through war.

---

[6] Santa Barbara Presidio Chapel, Baptism Book, #227.

[7] Carolyn Gale McGovern, *op. cit.*, p. 154.

THE CHANGING OF THE GUARD

In 1835, Mexican Texas had declared itself an independent republic. It was formally annexed to the United States in 1845 in one of President Tyler's last acts as President. This caused a great deal of suspicion about America's intentions regarding California. For the last quarter century, the acquisition of California had been a policy of several American presidents. Acting for President James Monroe, Secretary of State John Quincy Adams had tried to secure California in the early 1820s. He did again as president in early 1827. Andrew Jackson made a similar attempt to gain California in the first year of his administration (1829), and again in 1835 and 1837.

In the fall of 1845, President Polk sent his representative John Slidell to Mexico. Slidell was supposed to offer Mexico $25,000,000 to accept the Rio Grande boundary with Texas and to sell New Mexico, Arizona, and California to the U.S. However, the President of Mexico, preoccupied with internal dissension and suspicious of American intentions, refused to see Slidell. Slidell returned home, telling Polk that Mexico needed to be "chastised."

In the meantime, Polk had ordered Major General Zachary Taylor, with 3,000 men under his command, to advance from the Nueces River to the Rio Grande. He reached the river in April 1846. A Mexican force crossed the river to meet him. On April 25, the small body of American cavalry was defeated by the superior Mexican force. This incident gave President Polk the pretext he needed. Claiming that Mexico had "invaded our territory and shed American blood on American soil," he asked Congress to declare war. They did so on May 13, 1846.

The Mexican-American War

Accounts of the Mexican-American War in California have been provided by Neil Harlow in his book *California Conquered* (published in 1982) and by Lisbeth Haas in her article, "War in California, 1846-1848" (which was published in Ramón A. Gutiérrez and Richard J. Orsi's *Contested Eden*).[8] These sources should be consulted for a detailed account of the events that took place in California between 1846 and 1848. Professor Haas described the end of hostilities in California as follows:[9]

> The war in California ended with the Treaty of Cahuenga, signed on January 13, 1847. The articles of capitulation provided every citizen with the same rights as United States citizens. Californios were all guaranteed the protection of their life and property and the right to unhindered movement and travel, and

---

[8] Lisbeth Haas, "War in California, 1846-1848," in Ramón A. Gutiérrez and Richard J. Orsi, *op. cit.*, pp. 331-355.

[9] *Ibid.*, p. 345.

the men pledged that they would not take up arms again for the duration of the war with Mexico.

After the fall of California in January, 1847, American naval forces moved on Baja California with the intention of annexing the peninsula. In July, the American navy commenced with the occupation of the Baja Peninsula, a move that met with significant resistance. In the meantime, United States troops entered Mexico City in September and occupied the capital while armistice talks took place.

The Treaty of Guadalupe Hidalgo

When the Treaty of Guadalupe Hidalgo was signed on February 2, 1848, Mexico handed over to the United States 525,000 square miles of land. Although the present states of California, Arizona, Nevada, New Mexico, Nevada, and Colorado were ceded by this treaty, the United States withdrew its demand for the annexation for Baja California. In compensation, the U.S. paid $15,000,000 for the land and met other financial obligations to Mexico.

Of the treaty's twenty-three articles, four defined the rights of Mexican citizens and Indian people in the territories. Californians were given the freedom to live in ceded territories as either American or Mexican citizens and their property was to be

THE CHANGING OF THE GUARD

"inviolably respected." Those Californians who chose to become Americans would be entitled to "the enjoyment of all the rights of citizens of the United States according to the principles of the constitutions."[10] On September 9, 1850, California would be admitted to the Union as its thirty-first state. The state was divided into 27 counties, including Santa Barbara County, which – up until 1873 – also included present-day Ventura County.

In 1850, the large family of José Dolores Olivas – now American citizens – was enumerated in the United States Federal Census. José Delores Olivas gave his age was 48 years, while Gertrudis – erroneously listed as "Catarina" – stated that she was 38 years old. Their ten children – and their respective ages – were listed as follows: Juana (female, 18), María Antonia (female, 15), Susanna (female, 15), Guillermo (male, 13), José Victoriano (male, 12), Isabel (female, 10), Ramona (female, 9), Carolina (female, 8), and Felipe (male, 5), and José de los Santos (male, 3). All the members of the family were listed as natives of California.

It is believed that José Dolores died before 1860. In the 1860 federal census, Gertrudes Olivas was listed as the 40-year-old head of household in Dwelling 183 of the Santa Barbara Township in

---

[10] *Ibid.*, pp. 346-347.

THE CHANGING OF THE GUARD

Santa Barbara County. Nine of Gertrudis' children were still living at home at the time of this census.

María Antonia Olivas de Esquivel

María Antonia Olivas was born in February 1834 as the daughter of José Dolores Olivas and Gertrudis Valenzuela, the great-granddaughter of four *soldados de cuera* (Juan Matias Olivas, José Rosalino Fernández, Peter Gabriel Valenzuela, and Anastacio María Feliz), and the descendant of five pioneer California families. On November 30, 1849, María Antonia Olivas was married to José Apolinario Esquivel, a native of Irapuato, Guanajuato, Mexico, at the Santa Barbara Mission. The witnesses to this marriage were Joaquin and Josepha Valdés.[11]

On the following page we have produced a pedigree chart that indicates the ancestors of Maria Antonia Olivas and her descent from the four soldados who originally came to California (Juan Matias Olivas, José Rosalino Fernandez, Pedro Gabriel Valenzuela, and Anastacio Feliz).

---

[11] Santa Barbara Mission, Marriage Book, Number 324, November 30, 1849.

THE CHANGING OF THE GUARD

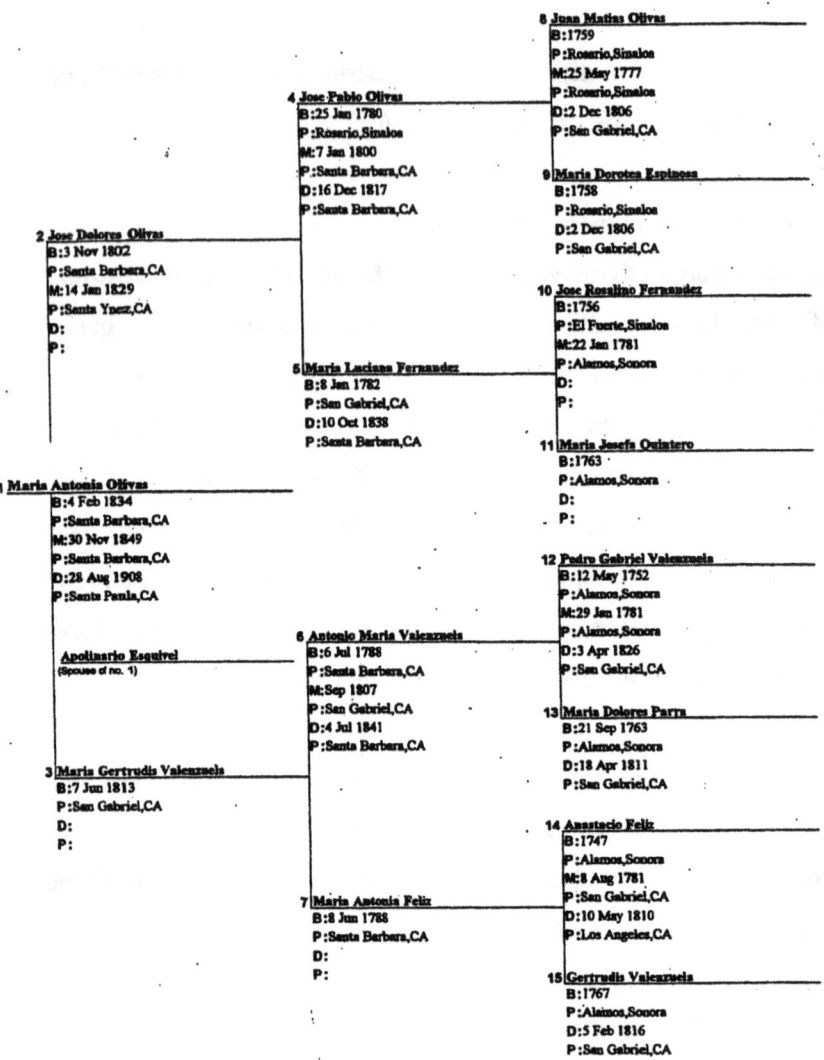

The Ancestors of María Antonia Olivas

THE CHANGING OF THE GUARD

On June 25, 1860, the federal census-taker arrived at the home of Apolinario Esquivel and asked questions that were required by law for all residents of the United States. Residing at Dwelling #67 of San Buenaventura Township in Santa Barbara County, 50-year-old "Polinario Escivi" was listed as a Mexican laborer who owned $250 of real estate and $300 of personal estate. His 30-year-old wife, María Antonia, was erroneously listed as "Malinta." Their six daughters were tallied as follows: Regina (10 years old), María (8), Francesca (6), Eloise (4), and the two twins: Ramona (3) and Francisca (3).

When the American Civil War broke out in 1861, the allegiance of Mexican Americans, particularly those living in Texas, was deeply divided. Initially, some 2,500 Mexican-American citizens went to war for the Confederacy, while 950 volunteered for service in the Union Army. By the end of this bloody struggle (1865), almost 10,000 Mexican Americans had served in regular army or volunteer units. Of the 40,000 books and pamphlets written about the Civil War, only one book *Vaqueros in Blue and Gray*, has been published about the role of Mexican Americans.[12]

---

[12] Jerry D. Thompson, *Vaqueros in Blue and Gray* (Austin, TX: Presidial Press, 1976).

THE CHANGING OF THE GUARD

As the war between the states raged in 1863, a call was sent out to the people of California to guard the West from Confederate incursions. At this time, the U.S. Government established four companies of Mexican-American Californians in order to utilize their "extraordinary horsemanship." Company C of the First California Native Cavalry was organized under Captain Antonio María de la Guerra. On July 24, 1864, José Victoriano Olivas, the younger brother of María Antonia Olivas, enlisted in this company which was made up of native troopers from Santa Barbara County.

Apolinario and María Antonia Esquivel lived for the rest of their lives in San Buenaventura Township of Santa Barbara County. Apolinario worked as a farmer and managed to accumulate a little extra cash. On January 28, 1886, Apolinario Esquivel died at an advanced age. On August 28, 1908, María A. Esquivel died in Santa Paula from a tumor.

THE ORTEGA FAMILY

In their sense of identity every people molds a vessel into which they pour from generation to generation the meanings of their historical experiences. Each such creation is for every enduring people a summation of the meaning and purpose of life. The spirit of a people cannot be known through a mere recitation of their customs; in such a listing the vital dimension is not present. This dimension is the people's feeling about the way they have performed and the values they have stood for in the course of their life history as a people. Such associations with real events in which people have suffered and triumphed are poured into the mold of identity and so come to have significance.[1]

An American Citizen

Regina Esquivel was born in 1851 as the daughter of José Apolinario Esquivel and María Antonia Olivas. She was the first member of her family to be born an American citizen. On January 3, 1870, Father Juan Comapla joined Regina Esquivel in marriage with Gregorio Ortega at the San Buenaventura Mission.[2] Gregorio Ortega had immigrated to the United States from southern Mexico sometime in the 1860s.

---

[1] Excerpt from *The Yaquis: A Cultural History* by Edward H. Spicer (Tucson, Arizona: The University of Arizona Press, 1980), p. 360. © 1980 The Arizona Board of Regents. Reprinted by permission of the University of Arizona Press.

[2] Certificate of Marriage, Ventura County Recorder's Office, filed for record, January 31, 1870.

THE ORTEGA FAMILY

Although Regina was listed in the household of her parents in the 1870 Federal census, she was also listed with her husband in his household. Gregorio was listed as a 25-year-old day laborer in San Buenaventura Township. Their first-born, child, Solomon, was listed as a year old.

During the 1870s, the Esquivel and Ortega families moved to a small farming community seven miles east of Ventura. In 1875, a Jewish merchant named Simon Cohn had opened a store in the area and, as a result, was called the founder of the small town which – at one point – was called New Jerusalem. Over the years, the small community had evolved from "The Corner" to "Cornerville," then to "Centerville," and to "New Jerusalem" in 1882.

In 1895, New Jerusalem became first Jerusalem and, finally, El Rio (The River). But long-time residents of Mexican-American descent are quick to say – with great pride – "To us, the place was always El Rio!"[3]

---

[3] Catherine Mervyn and Santa Clara Church, *A Tower in the Valley: The History of Santa Clara Church* (Tappan, NY: Custombook, 1989), p. 13.

THE ORTEGA FAMILY

In the 1860s and 1870s, people and businesses had begun to abbreviate San Buenaventura to S.B. Ventura. Katherine Van Dellen quoted this advice from the Inyo Independent newspaper, circa 1871: "...if they [the people of San Buenaventura] want to do a good thing for themselves, they will at once make a reduction on the name of their town. It's outrageous in this hurry skurry age to have to stop to write or speak such a name as that. No man in a hurry can do it and preserve his equanimity. This advice is free, entirely so."[4] In time, only the mission would still carry the name San Buenaventura.

Gregorio Ortega

In the Federal Census of 1880, Gregorio Ortega was listed as the forty-year-old head of household in the Ventura Township in Ventura County, California. Regina Ortega was 30 years old and gave California as her place of birth. Their children listed were: María A. (daughter, 10 years old), Solomon (son, 9 years old), Gregorio (son, 8), María L. (daughter, 6), Valentine (son, 5), Marcelina (daughter, 4), Genevive (daughter, 3), Michaela (daughter, 2), and Dionisio (son, two months old).

---

[4] Nancy S. Cloutier and Ann D. Snider, *The Ventura County and Coast Almanac* (Oxnard, California: Gold Coast Publications, 1988).

THE ORTEGA FAMILY

Forty-year-old Regina Esquivel died on April 23, 1891 after having given birth to a total of 18 children. Although a resident of New Jerusalem at the time, Regina's services were held at the San Bueanaventura Mission on April 25th.

In the 1900 Federal Census, Gregorio Ortega was listed as the head of a household of ten in Hueneme Township. Gregorio gave his age as 45 years and listed his date of birth as 1855, which is believed to be off by about 30 years. Although a native of Mexico, Gregorio stated that he was a naturalized citizen.

The children of Gregorio were listed as follows: Lucy Ortega (daughter, born December 1881, 18 years old); Clara (daughter, born June 1886, 13 years old); Isabel (daughter, born June 1883, 16 years old); Carrie (daughter, born March 1879, 21 years old); Jose (son, born November 1880, 19 years old); John (son, born June 1888, 11 years old); and Thomas (son, born November 1890, 9 years old). All of his children were listed as natives of California. Also living with him were a niece and a nephew, Willie Martinez (born August 1891, 8 years old) and Fidele Martinez (born August 1895, 4 years old).

Gregorio Ortega died of a cerebral hemorrhage on February 22, 1916 at the approximate age of 78 years. Gregorio had lost his

THE ORTEGA FAMILY

wife twenty-five years earlier and had retired to his home in El Rio. His funeral took place at Santa Clara Church, followed by burial in El Rio Cemetery.[5] The following obituary appeared in the Ventura Free Press after Gregorio's death:[6]

> PATRIARCH OF COUNTY DIES AT RIPE OLD AGE: Father of Eighteen Children and a Pioneer of County Passes Away Suddenly
>
> Gregorio Ortega, in his 75th year, was found cold in death at 7 o'clock Wednesday at his home in El Rio. He was sitting, fully dressed and with his hat on his head when found, and it was the opinion of the physician who was called that the old man had passed away early Tuesday evening.
>
> Ortega had eaten supper at the home of his son-in-law, David Ayala, early Tuesday evening and had gone directly to his rooms. It appeared that, on arriving there, he had sat himself on the edge of his bed, possibly for the purpose of disrobing for the night. He had thrown a light blanket about his shoulders.
>
> One of his daughters went to his room this morning to call him for breakfast and was not particularly surprised at finding him sitting on his couch dressed. But when he did not respond to her call she looked

---

[5] County of Ventura Death Certificate #190148, filed February 24, 1916.

[6] Ventura Free Press, February 25, 1916, p. 7.

more closely and thought her father asleep, or choking.

She removed his hat and eased his body into a reclining position and then discovered for the first time that life had fled. An Oxnard physician was called. Later Coroner Hathaway was summoned and later he convened an inquest. It was the verdict of the jury that death of Gregorio Ortega was due to an apoplectic stroke.

Ortega, a pioneer of the El Rio section, was the father of 18 children, fifteen of whom, eight sons and seven daughters, survive him. He was a sturdy character, a hard worker and a good citizen. Undertaker Diffenderffer of Oxnard is the undertaker in charge of the funeral arrangements.

Valentine Ortega and Theodora Tapia

Valentine Ortega was born on September 16, 1875 as the fifth child of Gregorio Ortega and Regina Esquivel. He was baptized shortly thereafter at San Buenaventura Mission, which his ancestors had founded in 1782. On October 7, 1893, 21-year-old Valentine Ortega was joined in marriage with 18-year-old Theodora Tapia by Father William A. Gains in Compton, California. The affidavit for marriage license stated that both were natives of California and residents of Compton.[7]

---

[7] Affidavit for Marriage License, Los Angeles County, No. 878, October 1893; Marriage license filed in Book 34, Page 12.

THE ORTEGA FAMILY

On November 30, 1876, María Marta Tapia Garcia had been baptized at Our Lady Queen of Angeles Catholic Church in Los Angeles. Her parents were listed as Juan Tapia and Celedonia Garcia. In the 1880 Federal Census, four-year old Teodora Tapia was listed in the household of her parents. The 36-year-old laborer, Juan Tapia, was living on San Gabriel Road in Los Angeles County. His young wife, Soledad, was only 18 years old. They had four daughters who were listed as follows: María A. (5 years old); Teodora (4); Lucia (2 years old), and Francisca (two months old).

Through my Tapia ancestors, I have inherited membership in the Chumash Indian Tribe. My family belongs to the Saticoy Branch of the Chumash Nation and many of us have taken an interest in customs of the Chumash in an attempt to understand the culture of our ancestors.

Valentine and Theodora moved to Ventura County in 1896. It was here that Valentine would find work as an agricultural laborer in the same fields worked by his father, Gregorio Ortega, and his grandfather, José Apolinario Esquivel. The very rich soil of the Oxnard Plains, combined with the mild climate, permitted the growth of a wide variety of crops, especially barley, beans, and beets. The nearby deepwater port in Hueneme had been

THE ORTEGA FAMILY

constructed in order to provide the farmers with an outlet for their agricultural products. Over time, the Oxnard/El Rio/Saticoy area would become one of the major agricultural areas in the state, as intensified row crop farming became popular in that district.

In the 1900 census, the young family of Valentine and Theodora Ortega lived in Hueneme Township, Ventura County, right next door to Valentine's father, Gregorio. Listed as a 26-year-old laborer who was born in February 1874 in California, Valentine stated that he had been married to his wife for six years. Theodora was listed as Valentine's 24-year-old wife who had given birth to a total of four children, two of whom were still living. Also listed in the household were their two daughters: Barbara (born March 1897) and Nevis (born August 1899).

In the 1910 Federal census, Valentine and his family still lived in the Hueneme Township of Ventura County. By this time, Valentine was 36 years of age and still listed his occupation as laborer. He stated that he had been married to his wife for 15 years and that he was a native-born Californian. Theodora M. Ortega was listed as Valentine's 34-year-old wife. In the last fifteen years, Theodora stated that she had given birth to a total of eight children, five of whom were still living. Their five children were listed with their respective ages as follows: Barbara G.

THE ORTEGA FAMILY

(female, 12); Felix V. (son, 8); Isabel (female, 6); Paz M. (female, 4); and Luciano P. (son, 2).

In 1918, at the forty-three years of age, Valentine Ortega fell victim to the world-wide influenza epidemic that ravaged the American continent in the months immediately following World War I. He was buried in Santa Clara Cemetery. Two years later, in the 1920 census, Theodora, now a widow, was the head of their household in Saticoy Village. Living in Enumeration District 273 of Ventura Township on January 10, 1920, she was classified as a forty-year-old native of California. Five children were listed in her household: Paz (daughter, 14); Luciano (son, 11), Sonjie (son, 9); Luz (daughter, 7); and Christina (daughter, 3). Living next door was her recently married daughter Isabel Sandoval with her husband and infant son.

As a young widow, Theodora was forced to raise her family by working odd jobs and with the generous help of her relatives. On Wednesday, August 3, 1965, Theodora Martha Ortega died in an Oxnard hospital at the age of 88. Theodora was survived by one son, Valentine Ortega, Jr. (who lived in Oxnard), as well as four daughters: Mrs. Isabel Melendez (the great-grandmother of Jennifer Vo), Mrs. Paz Orrante, Mrs. Lucy Flores, and Mrs. Christina Martinez, all of whom lived in Saticoy. She was also

THE ORTEGA FAMILY

survived by her brother John Corona (from Sacramento); a sister, Mrs. Frances Hernandez (of San Jose); 38 grandchildren; 89 great-grandchildren; and 15 great-great-grandchildren. Theodora's rosary was recited Thursday, August 5, 1965 at the Ted Mayr Loma Vista Chapel. On the following day, her funeral was held at Sacred Heart Catholic Church, followed by burial at Santa Clara Cemetery.[8]

Isabel Ortega and Refugio Gonzalez Melendez
Isabel was born on January 3, 1902 in Saticoy as the daughter of Valentine Ortega and Theodora Martha Tapia. On February 14, 1918, I.B. Martin, justice of the peace of the Santa Paula Township, joined 30-year-old Cleofas Sandobal in marriage with 15-year-old, Isabel Ortega.[9] Cleofas Sandoval had been born on May 1, 1889 in Mexico as the son of Leonidas Sandoval and Prisciliana Magyona, and had come to California in 1909 as a farm laborer. At the time of his marriage, he was a resident of Los Alamos, California. Not long after their marriage, Isabel gave birth to their first-born child, Valentine Sandoval.

---

[8] The Press-Courier, Wednesday, August 4, 1965.

[9] County of Ventura Marriage Record #194600.

THE ORTEGA FAMILY

In the 1920 federal census, Cleofas and Isabel were enumerated in Saticoy in the dwelling next door to Isabel's mother, Theodora Ortega. Cleofas was listed as a 37-year-old common laborer and a native of Mexico. At the time of the census, Isabel was 16 years of age and their son Valentine was only a year old. In the next few years, Cleofas and Isabel had two more children: Gregory and María Louisa. Their plans were brought to an end on May 10, 1924, when Cleofas Sandoval died from cardiac paralysis. It is believed that Cleofas had been ill with the flu and pharyngeal and laryngeal diphtheria were listed as contributory causes of death.

Shortly after the death of Cleofas, Isabel married her second husband, Marcos Hernandez. This short-lived marriage produced a son named Leonardo Hernandez. Sometime around 1926, Isabel met an immigrant laborer from Penjamo, Guanajuato, Mexico. The laborer, Refugio Melendez y Gonzalez had been born on July 4, 1893 as the only child of Ignacio Melendez and Angela Gonzalez. Refugio came to the United States in 1914 during the height of the Mexican Revolution.

The relationship between Isabel and Refugio got off to a rocky start. Their first-born child, Theodora – my maternal grandmother – was born in November 1927 at a time when they had split up

THE ORTEGA FAMILY

briefly. As a result, Dora was sent to live with her godparents, Casimiro and Refugio Delarosa.

Refugio was a docile, gentle person who found great enjoyment in gardening. Isabel, on the other hand, thrived on household chores such as plumbing, carpentry and electrical work. She raised chickens, goats, pigs, and canaries. According to her youngest daughter, Eva, Isabel was a woman who "was born before her time." During the depression years of the 1930s, both Refugio and Isabel had to go to work to make ends meet. While Isabel worked at a packing house in Saticoy, Refugio worked at a nearby ranch as an agricultural laborer. In this time, they would have six more children: Raymundo, Simon, Angela, Jacoba, Donald, and Eva. On April 25, 1956, 63-year-old Refugio Gonzales Melendez was officially married to 53-year-old Isabel Ortega Hernandez at the Santa Barbara Municipal Court.[10]

On Tuesday, October 27, 1964, Refugio died at Bellinda Hospital in Saticoy from coronary thrombosis. In the last of twenty years of his life, Refugio had been employed as an agricultural laborer by the Lloyd Corporation. He was survived by his wife, Isabel, and six daughters: Mrs. Mary Martinez (of Santa Paula), Mrs.

---

[10] Santa Barbara County Registry of Marriage, Book 1300, Page 550, No. 8136.

THE ORTEGA FAMILY

Mary Lou Vasquez (of Oxnard), Mrs. Angela Ayala (of Oxnard), Mrs. Dora Basultos (of San Fernando), Mrs. Eva Hubbert (of Ojai), and Mrs. Jobie Perez (of Saticoy). He was also survived by three sons, Simon Melendez (of Ventura); Ray Melendez (stationed with the U.S. Army in Germany), and Donald Melendez (of the U.S. Army in Florida); as well as 41 grandchildren and 7 great-grandchildren. Finally, he had three stepsons, Valentine Sandoval (of San Jose), Gregory Sandoval (of Saticoy), and Leonard Martinez (of Ventura). His funeral was held at Payton Mortuary in Oxnard. Burial was in Santa Clara Cemetery in Oxnard.[11]

On November 18, 1979, Isabel Ortega Melendez died at the Pacoima Community Hospital. The immediate cause of death was acute and chronic renal failure resulting from years of struggling with diabetes mellitus. At the time of death, she had resided at 11339 Aster Street in Saticoy, the residence of her son, Gregory Sandoval.

---

[11] The Press-Courier, Wednesday, October 28, 1964.

IN THE SERVICE OF THEIR COUNTRY

Hispanic Americans have defended our nation with pride and courage. Thirty-seven Hispanic Americans have received the Medal of Honor – America's highest military decoration for valor.[1]

The Korean Conflict saw many Hispanic Americans again respond to the call of duty. They served with distinction in all of the services.... Many Mexican Americans from barrios in Los Angeles, San Antonio, Laredo, Phoenix, and Chicago saw fierce action in Korea. Fighting in almost every combat unit in Korea, they distinguished themselves through courage and bravery as they had in previous wars.[2]

Mexican-American Contributions to Freedom

As Mexican-American citizens of California, my family has carried on a proud tradition of military service. When our nation has been in need, my ancestors – from the earliest days in California – answered the call with a sense of pride and obligation. This sense of duty is a deeply held tradition to all Mexican-Americans.

According to the United States Department of Defense publication, *Hispanics in America's Defense*, "when our country has been in need, Hispanic Americans have had more than their

---

[1] Office of the Deputy Assistant Secretary of Defense for Military Manpower and Personnel Policy, U.S. Department of Defense, *Hispanics in America's Defense* (Collingdale, Pennsylvania: Diane Publishing Co., 1997), p. 3

[2] *Ibid.*, p. 33.

IN THE SERVICE OF THEIR COUNTRY

share of stouthearted, indomitable men. Their intrepid actions have been in the highest tradition – a credit to themselves, their ancestry, and our nation."[3]

At the time of America's entry into World War II (1941), approximately 2,690,000 Americans of Mexican ancestry lived in the United States. Eighty-five percent of this population lived in the five southwestern states (California, Arizona, New Mexico, Texas, and Colorado). In 1940, while America was still at peace, two National Guard units from New Mexico, the 200th and 515th Coast Artillery (Anti-aircraft) battalions were activated and dispatched to the Philippine Islands. Largely made up of Spanish-speaking personnel – both officers and enlisted men from New Mexico, Arizona, and Texas – the two units were stationed at Clark Field, 65 miles from Manila.

On December 7, 1941, the Japanese Imperial Navy launched a surprise attack on the American naval fleet at Pearl Harbor, forcing America into war. Within days, Japanese forces attacked the American positions in the Philippines. Outnumbered and desperate, General Douglas MacArthur moved his forces, including the 200th and 515th, to the Bataan Peninsula west of

---

[3] *Ibid.*, p. 49

IN THE SERVICE OF THEIR COUNTRY

Manila. Here, fighting alongside their Filipino comrades, they made a heroic three-month stand against the large, well-equipped invading forces. As the weeks wore on, rations, medical supplies, and ammunition became scarce.

On April 9, 1942, starving and greatly outnumbered, most of the surviving troops surrendered. After their capture, the American and Filipino soldiers had to endure the 12-day, 85-mile "death march" from Bataan to the death camps, followed by 34 months of captivity. Three years later, General Jonathan Wainwright praised the men of the 200th and 515th units, saying that "they were the first to fire and the last to lay down their arms and only reluctantly doing so after being given a direct order."[4]

In the Pacific theater, the 158th Regimental Combat Team, known as the *Bushmasters*, an Arizona National Guard unit comprised of many Mexican-American soldiers, saw heavy combat. They earned the respect of General MacArthur who referred to them as "the greatest fighting combat team ever deployed for battle." Company E of the 141st Regiment of the 36th Texas Infantry Division was made entirely of Spanish-speaking Americans, the majority of them from Texas. After 361 days of combat in Italy

---

[4] *Ibid.*, pp. 27-28.

and France, the 141st Infantry Regiment sustained 1,126 killed, 5,000 wounded, and over 500 missing in action. In recognition of their extended service and valor, the members of the 141st garnered 31 Distinguished Service Crosses, 12 Legion of Merits, 492 Silver Stars, 11 Soldier's Medals, 1,685 Bronze Stars, as well as numerous commendations and decorations. In all, twelve Hispanic soldiers received the Medal of Honor for their services during World War II.[5]

The Korean War

When the Korean War began in 1950, young Americans received another call to arms. The three sons of Refugio and Isabel Melendez – my grand uncles – answered the call and served alongside other American boys in this Asian war. Simon, Donald, and Raymundo Melendez eventually served during or shortly after the three-year Asian war.

Uncle Simon's career in the military was certainly a distinguished one. Born October 28, 1930, Simon Melendez was raised in Saticoy and attended Ventura Junior High School and Ventura City College. When the Korean War started, Simon joined the 2nd Division of the U.S. Army and became a machine gunner.

---

[5] *Ibid.*, p. 29

IN THE SERVICE OF THEIR COUNTRY

Uncle Simon took part in two of the bloodiest battles of the Korean War. The "Battle of Bloody Ridge" began in August 1951 and continued up until September 12, 1951. On August 27, Simon was hit in the neck and legs by mortar shrapnel and in the back by grenade fragments. At the same time, he was separated from his platoon. For seven days, he was behind enemy lines, stuck in torrential rains that made his weapon inoperable.

The rain did not stop until the sixth day, and on the seventh day he was able to make his way into the area of the 9th Regiment. When asked how he managed to make his way through enemy lines for seven days, 21-year-old Simon explained that "my extreme faith in God brought me through."

Not long after this, Simon was able to have a three-day reunion with his brother Raymond Melendez near the front lines. Raymond, who had already been in the service for six years, was a paratrooper and had been stationed about a 100 miles from Simon's position. Soon after, Simon was once again in the thick of the fighting when his unit took part in the "Battle of Heartbreak Ridge," which lasted from September 13 to October 22, 1951.

The Battles of Bloody Ridge and Heartbreak Ridge were the two bloodiest battles of the Korean War. By the time he left the service, Simon had been awarded the Silver Star, the Bronze Star, and three Purple Hearts. He also founded the Mexican-American Korean War Veterans of Ventura County and became a life member of the Veterans of Foreign Wars and the American Legion.

Uncle Simon returned home to get married in 1953 and to begin working for the Southern California Gas Company. After forty years of service, he retired. Simon Melendez, the proud Korean War veteran, died at the age of 71 on June 15, 2002, surrounded by his loved ones.

Vietnam

During the extended Vietnam Conflict (1963-1973), approximately 80,000 Hispanic Americans served in the American military. Although Hispanics made up only about 4.5% of the total U.S. population at that time, they incurred more than 19% of the casualties. In all, thirteen Hispanic soldiers received the Medal of Honor during this conflict.

Continuing this trend of service into the last decade of the Twentieth Century, twenty thousand Hispanic servicemen and women participated in Operation Desert Shield and Desert Storm (1990-1991). Writing in *Hispanic Heritage Month 1996:*

IN THE SERVICE OF THEIR COUNTRY

Hispanics – Challenging the Future, Army Chaplain (Captain) Carlos C. Huerta of the First Battalion, 79th Field Artillery stated that "Hispanics have always met the challenge of serving the nation with great fervor. In every war, in every battle, on every battlefield, Hispanics have put their lives on the line to protect freedom."

THE LATER GENERATIONS

When my grandfather Refugio died in 1964, I was a teenager. After attending his funeral, my family went to the Santa Clara Cemetery [in Oxnard]. Once the service had ended, my Uncle Simon [Melendez] took me for a walk through the cemetery. We moved from one tombstone to another as my uncle pointed out the gravestones for many of my ancestors. He showed me where Gregorio and Valentine Ortega were buried, as well as other family members. As we walked, Uncle Simon explained to me that our family had been in California for a very long time. For him, this was a great source of pride. He especially touched me when he said, "Our family has known no home but California. This is where we belong."[1]

Theodora Ortega Melendez

My maternal grandmother, Theodora Melendez was born on November 9, 1927 in Saticoy, Ventura County, California, as the first-born child of Refugio Melendez and Isabel Ortega. However, at this time, her parents were not married, and, in fact, the two had recently broken up. For this reason, the infant Theodora was brought to live in Simi Valley with her godparents, Casimiro and Refugio dela Rosa. On October 21, 1928, little Dora was baptized at Santa Rosa de Lima Catholic Church in Simi Valley.

Dora attended first grade in Simi Valley. However, in the following year, Casimiro moved his small family to the San Fernando Valley where Dora, at the age of 7, started school at the San Fernando Elementary School. During the darkest years of the Great

---

[1] A quote from Sarah Basulto Evans (mother of Jennifer Vo).

THE LATER GENERATIONS

Depression, Casimiro worked as a shoe repairman while Refugio cared for little Dora.

In 1948, Dora met Eusebio Basulto, a young migrant worker from Ocotlán, Jalisco. Two years earlier, Eusebio had crossed the border into California to work as a laborer. Dora and Eusebio were married and on January 24, 1949, Dora gave birth to their first-born child, Sarah Paz Basulto.

Eleven months later, on December 23, 1949, Dora would provide Sarah with a little sister, who was named Franceska Victoria María. It was not long after this that Eusebio and Dora separated. But in 1952, Eusebio returned and they tried to make a life together one more time. Their third child, Eusebio Javier Antonio Basulto, was born on October 5, 1953 in the San Fernando Valley. Shortly after this, Dora and Eusebio separated for the last time.

As a young woman, Dora got her first job at the Burmide Flare Company. A couple of years later, she moved on to Pacific Mercury where she worked as a machinist. Through training sessions and experience, she became a riveter and helped to produce many of the earliest television sets of the 1950s. As a single mother of three children in the early 1960s, Dora found it necessary to move on to her next position as a machine operator at Withrow Die Casting. In 1979, she went to school to learn advanced machinist techniques. After a period of training, Dora started a new job as an electronic machinist at Rentec. She continued to work there until her retirement in 1991.

Dora worked hard to raise her family alone. Sometimes she found it necessary to take a second job to put food on the dinner table. As a means of making a better life for herself and her children, Dora sought to learn more skills through training programs. And she instilled in her children an understanding of the value of education. She encouraged all three of her children – and her grandchildren – to finish high school and supported their efforts to continue their education at the local colleges.

In the tradition of her hard-working ancestors, Dora has always striven to do a good job no matter what. Even after her retirement, she took on a part-time job in the cafeteria at the San Fernando High School. Dora loves to bowl and to dance and spends a great deal of her spare time in these activities.

Sarah Basulto
Theodora and Eusebio's eldest daughter, Sarah Paz Basulto, is my mother. As the great-great-great-great-great-great-great-granddaughter of Luis Quintero, Sarah qualifies as a tenth-generation Californian. Born on January 24, 1949 as the daughter of Eusebio

THE LATER GENERATIONS

Basulto and Theodora Ortega Melendez, Mother grew up in the Sylmar district of the San Fernando Valley. While attending high school at Sylmar High School, the teen-aged Sarah met David Charles Kunkel, who would eventually become her first husband.

David Charles Kunkel had been born on May 24, 1949 in Grand Prairie, Texas as the son of Roland Kunkel and Josephine Fowler. David Kunkel was a descendant of both German immigrants and of several old Southern American families. His great-grandfather, Albert O. Kunkel, had immigrated from Germany in 1874 when he was only 15 years of age. Landing at Galveston, Texas, the Kunkel family had settled at Shive, Hamilton County, Texas, as one of that area's pioneer families.

Albert O. Kunkel's son, Albert Julius Max Kunkel, was born on February 16, 1896 in Clifton, Bosque County, Texas. On December 15, 1916, Albert Julius was married to Nettie Jane Appleby, the daughter of James Thomas Appleby and Bell Ross Jones. Albert and Nettie's first-born child, Roland Lee Kunkel, was born on March 9, 1918 in Shive. With the outbreak of war in 1917, Albert soon joined the U.S. Army. Although Roland Lee was of German descent through his father, he was also of old American lineage through his Appleby and Jones ancestors. Roland was the eldest of eight children and, like his father, served in the military (during World War II).

THE LATER GENERATIONS

Roland Lee Kunkel was married in the late 1940s to Edith Josephine Fowler. They had three sons: Roland (Ron) Lee, Jr., David Charles, and Dennis James. When David Charles was still quite young, his parents moved their family west to Sylmar, California.

Shortly after my mother graduated from Sylmar High in 1967, she and David decided to get married. They were married in Newhall, California and settled down to raise their family in Sylmar. I, Jennifer Celeste Kunkel, was their firstborn child. I was born on March 12, 1968. While David worked as a remelt operator at Withrow Die Casting, Sarah took care of their daughter, Jennifer. However, starting in 1971, Sarah decided to attend Valley College in North Hollywood. In the years to follow, even after going to work full-time, Sarah continued to pursue her studies.

Initially, Sarah studied mechanical technology and quality engineering at Pierce College in Woodland Hills. However, a few years later, she started to concentrate her efforts in Early Childhood Development. In 1979, she obtained her AA degree in Education with a specialty in Early Childhood Development. On January 31, 1973, Sarah and David had their second child, Tara Delarosa Kunkel. Shortly after this, David and Sarah were divorced.

THE LATER GENERATIONS

As a single mother of two daughters, Sarah continued to work full-time and pursue her studies. In 1979, went to work as a quality assurance manager at an electronics manufacturer in the San Fernando Valley. She continues to work there today. However, while attending Valley College, Sarah met Floyd Ray Evans, an electronic engineering student who had been born on January 29, 1949 in Mount Holly, New Jersey. On November 1988, Sarah and Floyd were married in Reno, Nevada. On May 3, 1989, Sarah gave birth to twins: Michael John Evans and Amanda Kate Evans.

When he was twenty years old, Eusebio Javier Antonio Basulto followed in the family's military tradition and enlisted in the Army. After several years of active duty, Eusebio became a military reservist and took a job as a chemist.

AN AMERICAN EXPERIENCE

The past 30 years have simply repeated the process of mestizaje that began more than 100 years ago, when Spanish, Mexican, and Indian peoples each relinquished concepts of racial purity in favor of cultural transformation. The Chicano of the 1970s and 1980s stands as the newest reflection of a community that has always chosen from its myriad influences the elements of culture that best suit its immediate needs. No longer Indian but of the Indian, not Spanish but of Europe, Mexicans have emerged as the embodiment of all these cultures...

Overall, the last three decades have been filled with self-discovery for most U.S. Mexicans. They have found and exercised their strengths, solidified their own ground, and survived repeated attacks from within and without. Beyond all else, the last 30 years have shown them that they are an immovable force in Los Angeles and throughout the Southwest. Like every generation that has come before them, they are forging their path in new and unusual ways. What they will be tomorrow, they are shaping today.[1]

Jennifer Kunkel Vo

As the great-great-great-great-great-great-great-great-granddaughter of Luis Quintero, I am the eleventh generation to live in the present-day state of California. Born as Jennifer Celeste Kunkel on March 12, 1968, I was the first-born child of David Charles Kunkel and Sarah Basulto. My first vision of the world came from the rooms of the Granada Hills Hospital in the San Fernando Valley. Five years later on January 31, 1973, my parents provided me with a little sister, Tara Delarosa Kunkel.

---

[1] Rios-Bustamante and Castillo, *op. cit.*, p. 188.

AN AMERICAN EXPERIENCE

Growing up in Sylmar, I attended El Dorado Elementary School, after which I moved on to Olive Vista Middle School. At the age of 15, I was accepted as a student in the Mathematics/Science magnet program at Van Nuys High School. In addition to the required curriculum, I immersed herself in the music program at Van Nuys. By the time that I reached the seventh grade, I had learned to play the flute. Moving on to high school, my enthusiasm for music continued, so I decided to join the school's marching band. By the time that I had graduated from high school, I had joined the California Junior Philharmonic Orchestra and received the "Director's Award for Music."

It was during my high school years that I met the man who would later become her husband, James Vo. James Dung Vo was born on May 10, 1968 in Saigon, Vietnam. With his mother and siblings, James had fled the faltering South Vietnamese Republic in April of 1975. A month later, the Saigon Republic fell into the hands of the victorious Viet Cong forces. Once in America, James' family found a home in Sylmar. James very quickly learned English while attending Olmeveny Elementary School.

As he progressed into his teen years, James moved on to Olive Vista Middle School and then to Van Nuys High School. Both James and I were bussed from our respective homes in Sylmar to Van Nuys High.

Through this association, we became acquainted. By the time we were in our Senior Year, we had become good friends and attended the high school prom together.

In 1987, James and I both moved on to Cal State University at Northridge (CSUN). While I took English as my major, James decided on Computer Sciences as his course of study. Coincidentally, during our college years, we both started jobs at Magic Mountain in Valencia, California. It was around this time that our relationship took on a more serious nature and we began to date.

In 1991, I graduated from CSUN. James graduated a year later and took a position with Great Western Bank as a computer specialist. Both James and I were the first persons in their respective families to obtain bachelor's degrees from a four-year college. On October 16, 1993, we were married at St. Didacus Church in Sylmar. The best man was James' stepbrother, Alan Vela, and the maid of honor, Sheri Finkelstein.

After settling down to married life in Sylmar, I went to work for the Valley Village, a nonprofit organization that maintained homes for developmentally disabled adults. At the same time, James left his job at Great Western Bank to become a Distribution Clerk for the United States Postal Service.

AN AMERICAN EXPERIENCE

In October 1994, I became an editor at a publishing company in western part of the San Fernando Valley. It was at this time, that we decided to start a family. On September 27, 1995, I gave birth to Ryan James Vo at Holy Cross Hospital in Mission Hills. More than two years later, on January 6, 1998, we had a second child, Jessica Saramai Vo, would come into the world at the Granada Hills Hospital.

The Next Generation

My children, Ryan James and Jessica Saramai Vo, are truly products of the "American Melting Pot," as they have ancestors from four continents: Asia, North America, Africa, and Europe. Through their father, they are half Asian. Through my maternal grandfather, Eusebio Basulto, they have inherited one-eighth of their ancestry from the Mexican state of Jalisco. Through my father, they inherit English, Irish and German ancestry. I intend for them to be proud of their heritage as Americans, as Mexican-Americans, and as Asian-Americans.

But we live in the state of California, and our roots run very deep in this state. Our Chumash ancestors (from the Tapia family) lived as hunters and fisherman along the California Coast in what is present-day Santa Barbara County. In order to appreciate this connection, we have become officially affiliated with the Chumash tribal organization.

Ryan and Jessica represent the twelfth generation from Luis Quintero to live in the state of California. Luis Quintero – along with his wife and children – was with the group of people who first stepped foot inside of the new Pueblo of Los Angeles in 1781. Ten direct ancestors of mine (Juan Matias Olivas, María Dorotea Espinosa, José Rosalino Fernandez, María Josefa Quintero, Luis Quintero, María Petra Rubio, Pedro Gabriel Valenzuela, María Dolores Parra, Gertrudis Valenzuela, and José Pablo Olivas) traveled from Sonora, Mexico in the Expedition of 1781, which had been organized for the specific purpose of establishing the Presidio of Santa Barbara and the Pueblo of Los Angeles. And one ancestor, Anastacio María Feliz, arrived in California several years earlier.

Like their pioneer ancestors before them, my children have inherited a special destiny as they come of age in the New Millennium. And when they face the challenges of the Twenty-First Century, they will be able to look back with pride at their pioneer ancestors and the hardships and struggles that they endured.

BIBLIOGRAPHY

Adams, Richard E.W. *Prehistoric Mesoamerica.* Boston: Little, Brown and Company, Inc., 1977.

Atkinson, William C. *Spain: A Brief History.* London: Methuen & Co., 1934.

Bancroft, Hubert Howe. *History of Mexico: Volume III. 1600-1803.* San Francisco: A. L. Bancroft & Company, Publishers, 1883.

Bancroft, Hubert H. *History of California, Volume I, 1542-1800.* San Francisco: A.L. Bancroft & Company, Publishers, 1885.

Bancroft, Hubert H. *History of California, Volume II, 1801-1824.* Santa Barbara, California: Wallace Hebberd, 1966.

Bannon, John Francis. *The Spanish Borderlands Frontier, 1513-1821.* New York, 1970.

Benítez, Fernando. The Century After Cortéz. Chicago: The University of Chicago Press, 1965.

Benítez, Fernando. *Palou and his Writings.* Berkeley, 1926

Bolton, Herbert L. "The Mission as a Frontier Institution in the Spanish American Colonies," *American Historical Review,* 23:1 (October, 1917), 42-61.

Brinckerhoff, Sidney B. and Odie B. Faulk. *Lancers for the King: A Study of the Frontier Military System of Northern New Spain.* Phoenix, AZ, 1965.

BIBLIOGRAPHY

California Archives. *Provincial State Papers, 1767-1822.* Archives of California, Bancroft Library, U.C. Berkeley.

Camarillo, Albert. *Chicanos in California: A History of Mexican Americans in California.* Sparks, NV: Materials for Today's Learning, 1990.

Campbell, Leon G. "The Spanish Presidio in Alta California During the Mission Period 1769-1784", *The Journal of the West,* Vol. XVI, No. 4, October 1977, pp. 63-77.

Campbell, Leon G. "The First Californios: Presidial Society in Spanish California 1769-1822", *Journal of the West,* Vol. IX, No. 4, October 1972, pp. 582-595.

Chapman, Charles E. *The Alta California Supply Ships 1773-1776.* Austin, Texas: 1915

Chapman, Charles E. *A History of California: The Spanish Period.* New York: The MacMillan Company, 1921

Chapman, Charles E. *The Foundation of California, The Northwestern Expansion of New Spain, 1867-1783.* New York, 1916

Chávez, John R. *The Lost Land: The Chicano Image of the Southwest.* Albuquerque: University of New Mexico Press, 1984.

Cheetham, Sir Nicolas. *Mexico: A Short History.* New York: Thomas Y. Crowell Company, 1970.

BIBLIOGRAPHY

Christiansen, Paige W. "The Presidio and the Borderlands: A Case Study." *Journal of the West*, Vol. VIII, I (January 1969), pp. 29-37.

Cloutier, Nancy S. and Snider, Ann D. *The Ventura County and Coast Almanac.* Oxnard, California: Gold Coast Publications, 1988.

Cockcroft, James D. *Mexico: Class Formation, Capital Accumulation, and the State.* New York: Monthly Review Press, 1983.

Corwin, Arthur F. "Mexican Emigration History, 1900-1970: Literature and Research," *Latin American Research Review*, VIII (Summer 1973), 3-24.

Davies, Nigel. *The Aztecs: A History.* Norman, Oklahoma: University of Oklahoma, 1980.

Deeds, Susan M. "Indigenous Rebellions on the Northern Mexican Mission Frontier: From First-Generation to Later Colonial Responses," in Donna J. Guy and Thomas E. Sheridan (eds.), *Contested Ground: Comparative Frontiers on the Northern and Southern Edges of the Spanish Empire.* Tucson: University of Arizona Press, 1998.

Deeds, Susan M. "Indigenous Rebellions on the Northern Mexican Mission Frontier: From First-Generation to Later Colonial Responses," in Susan Schroeder, *Native Resistance and the Pax Colonial in New Spain.* Lincoln, Nebraska: University of Nebraska Press, 1998, pp. 1-29.

Denis, Alberta Johns. *Spanish Alta California.* New York: The MacMillan Company, 1927.

BIBLIOGRAPHY

Department of Defense. *The Hispanics in America's Defense.* Washington, D.C.: U.S. Printing Office, 1990.

Dobyns, Henry F. "Estimating Aboriginal American Population," *Current Anthropology 7* (1966), pp. 395-449.

Dunbier, Roger. *The Sonoran Desert. Its Geography, Economy and People.* Tucson, Arizona: University of Arizona Press. Tucson, Arizona, 1970.

Duran, Livie Isauro and H. Russell Bernard (eds.). *Introduction to Chicano Studies* (2nd edition). New York: Macmillan Publishing Co., Inc., 1982.

Elliott, J. H. *The Spanish World: Civilization and Empire, Europe and the Americas, Past and Present.* New York: Harry N. Abrams, Inc., 1991.

Engelhardt, Zepherim. *San Gabriel Mission and the Beginnings of Los Angeles.* San Gabriel: The James H. Barry Company, 1927.

Engelhardt, Zepherim. *Missions and Missionaries of California*, Vol. I-II. Santa Barbara, 1929-30.

Engstrand, Iris H.W. *San Diego: Father Junipero Serra and California's Beginnings.* San Diego, California: The San Diego Historical Society, 1982.

Ewing, Russell C. et al. *Six Faces of Mexico.* Tucson, Arizona: The University of Arizona Press, 1966.

Faulk, Odie B. "The Presidio: Fortress or Farce?" *Journal of the West*, Vol. VIII, No. 1 (January 1969), pp. 21-28.

BIBLIOGRAPHY

Funk & Wagnalls Corporation, *The World Almanac and Book of Facts*, 1995. Mahwah, New Jersey: Funk & Wagnalls Corporation, 1994.

Garr, Daniel J. *Hispanic Colonial Settlement in California: Planning and Urban Development on the Frontier, 1769-1850*. Cornell University, Ph.D. Thesis, 1971.

Geiger, Maynard. *The Life and Times of Fray Junipero Serra*, 2 Volumes. Washington, 1955.

Geiger, Maynard. *Mission Santa Barbara 1782-1965*. Santa Barbara, California: Heritage Printers, Inc., 1965.

Geiger, Maynard. "Six Census Records of Los Angeles and Its Immediate Area Between 1804 and 1823," *Southern California Quarterly,* Vol. LIV, No. 4, pp. 311-341.

Gerhard, Peter. *The Northern Frontier of New Spain*. Princeton, New Jersey: Princeton University Press, 1982.

Gutiérrez, Ramón and Orsi, Richard J. *Contested Eden: California Before the Gold Rush*. Berkeley: University of California Press, 1998.

Hanks, Patrick and Hodges, Flavia. *A Dictionary of Surnames*. Oxford: Oxford University Press, 1988.

Harlow, Neal. *California Conquered: War and Peace on the Pacific 1846-1850*. Berkeley, University of California Press, 1982.

Hauberg, Clifford A. *Puerto Rico and the Puerto Ricans*. New York: Twayne Publishers, Inc., 1974.

BIBLIOGRAPHY

Hawley, Walter A. *The Early Days of Santa Barbara.* Santa Barbara: Santa Barbara Heritage, 1987.

Jennings, Francis. *The Founders of America: How Indians Discovered The Land, Pioneered in it, and Created Great Classical Civilizations, How They Were Plunged Into a Dark Age by Invasion and Conquest, and How They Are Reviving.* New York: W. W. Norton & Company, Inc., 1993.

Jiménez, Carlos M. *The Mexican American Heritage.* Berkeley, California: TQS Publications, 1994 (2nd edition).

Jones, Oakah I. *Los Paisanos: Spanish Settlers on the Northern Frontier of New Spain.* Norman: University of Oklahoma Press, 1978.

Kaufman, Terrence Golla, Victor, "Language Groupings in the New World: Their Reliability and Usability in Cross-Disciplinary Studies," in Colin Renfrew (ed.), *America Past, America Present: Genes and Languages in the Americas and Beyond.* Cambridge: The McDonald Institute for Archaeological Research, 2000.

Layne, J. Gregg, "Annals of Los Angeles: Part I. From the Founding of the Pueblo to the American Occupation," *California Historical Society Quarterly,* Vol. XIII, No. 3 (September 1934), pp. 195-234.

Marks, Richard Lee. *Cortés: The Great Adventurer and the Fate of Aztec Mexico.* New York: Alfred A. Knopf, 1994.

Martinez y Romero, Evelyn. *My Family Back Bone: A Genealogy of Romero, Olivas, Cota, Pico, Eddy, & Story Families.* San Jose, California: Foothill Printers and Capitol Printing, 1984.

BIBLIOGRAPHY

Mason, Bill. "The Garrisons of San Diego Presidio, 1770-1794," *The Journal of San Diego History*, Vol. XXIV, No. 4 (Fall 1978).

Mason, J. Alden. "The Native Languages of Middle America," in *The Maya and Their Neighbors*. New York: D. Appleton-Century Company, 1949.

Mason, William Marvin. *The Census of 1790: A Demographic History of Colonial California.* Menlo Park, California: Ballena Press, 1998.

McDowell, Jack (ed.). *Mexico.* Menlo Park, California: Lane Magazine & Book Company, 1973.

McGovern, Carolyn Gale. *Hispanic Population in Alta California.* Unpublished Master's Thesis, California State University, Northridge, 1978.

Meier, Matt S. and Feliciano Rivera. *The Chicanos: A History of Mexican Americans*. New York: Hill and Wang, 1972.

Meier, Matt S. and Feliciano Ribera. *Mexican Americans, American Mexicans: From Conquistadors to Chicanos.* New York: Hill and Wang, 1993.

Mervyn, Catherine and Santa Clara Church. *A Tower in the Valley: The History of Santa Clara Church.* Tappan, NY: Custombook, 1989.

Meyer, Michael C. *The Course of Mexican History*. New York: Oxford University Press, 1987.

BIBLIOGRAPHY

Millon, René. "Teotihuacán: City, State and Civilization," in *Archaeology*, edited by Jeremy A. Sabloff and with assistance of Patricia A. Andrews, *Supplement to the Handbook of Middle American Indians, Vol. I*. Austin, Texas: University of Texas Press, 1981.

Moorhead, Max L. "The Soldado de Cuera: Stalwart of the Spanish Borderlands," *Journal of the West*, Vol. VIII, No. 1 (January 1969), pp. 38-55.

Newton, Linda, "Pre-Columbian Settlement," *Cambridge Encyclopedia of Latin America and the Caribbean*. New York: Cambridge University Press, 1985.

Nunis, Doyce B. (ed). *Southern California's Spanish Heritage: An Anthology*. Los Angeles: Historical Society of Southern California, 1992.

Office of the Deputy Assistant Secretary of Defense for Military Manpower and Personnel Policy. *Hispanics in America's Defense*. Collingdale, Pennsylvania: Diane Publishing Company, 1997.

O'Neill, Owen H. (ed.). *History of Santa Barbara County: Its People and Resources*. Santa Barbara: Harold MacLean Meier, 1939.

Parks, Marion. "Instructions for the Recruital of Soldiers and Settlers for California – Expedition of 1781," *Quarterly of the Historical Society of Southern California*, Vol. XV, Part II, 1931.

Phelan, Regina V. *The Land Known as Alta California*. Spokane: Prosperity Press, 1997.

BIBLIOGRAPHY

Priestley, Herbert Ingram. *The Mexican Nation, A History.* New York: The Macmillan Company, 1926.

Pryde, Philip R. *San Diego: An Introduction to the Region.* Dubuque, Iowa: Kendall/Hunt Publishing Co., 1976.

Radding, Cynthia. "The Colonial Pact and Changing Ethnic Frontiers in Highland Sonora, 1740-1840" in Donna J. Guy and Thomas E. Sheridan (eds.), *Contested Ground: Comparative Frontiers on the Northern and Southern Edges of the Spanish Empire*, pp. 52-66. Tucson: University of Arizona Press, 1998.

Ramos Wold, Lillian. *Hispanic Surnames: History and Genealogy.* Midway City, California: SHHAR Press, 1994.

Reff, Daniel T. *Depopulation, and Culture Change in Northwestern New Spain, 1518-1764.* Salt Lake City: University of Utah Press, 1991.

Rios-Bustamante, Antonio, and Pedro Castillo, *An Illustrated History of Mexican Los Angeles, 1781-1981.* Chicano Studies Research Center, Monograph #12, Los Angeles: University of California, Chicano Studies Research Center Publications, 1986.

Rios-Bustamante, Dr. Antonio. *Mexican Los Angeles.* Encino, Califonria: Floricanto Press. 1992.

Robinson, W.W. *Los Angeles: From the Days of the Pueblo.* Revised: North Hollywood: California Historical Society, 1981.

Sanchez, George. *Becoming Mexican American.* New York: Oxford University Press. 1993.

BIBLIOGRAPHY

Schmal, John P. "The History of Hispanics in America's Defense," www.somosprimos.com (July 2000, Issue 7).

Schneidau, Barbara. *A Guide to Old Santa Barbara: The Spanish & Mexican Periods*. Goleta: Triple R Press, 1977.

Security Trust & Savings Bank. *El Pueblo: Los Angeles Before the Railroads*. Los Angeles, 1928.

Simpson, Lesley Byrd. *Many Mexicos*. Berkeley, California: University of California Press, 1971.

Smith, Michael E. *The Aztecs*. Cambridge, Massachusetts: Blackwell Publishers, Inc., 1996.

Salmon, Robert Mario. *Indian Revolts in Northern New Spain: A Synthesis of Resistance (1680-1786)*. Lanham, Maryland: University Press of America, Inc., 1991.

Spicer, Edward H. "Ways of Life" in Russell C. Ewing et al. *Six Faces of Mexico*. The University of Arizona Press, 1966.

Spicer, Edward H. *Cycles of Conquest: The Impact of Spain, Mexico, and the United States on the Indians of the Southwest, 1533-1960*. Tucson, Arizona: University of Arizona Press, 1997.

Spicer, Edward H. *The Yaquis: A Cultural History*. Tucson, Arizona: The University of Arizona Press, 1980.

Staniford, Edward F. *The Pattern of California History*. New York: Canfield Press, 1975.

Stevens, Meredith. *The House of Olivas*. Ventura, California: Charon Press.

BIBLIOGRAPHY

Temple, Thomas Workman. "Soldiers and Settlers of the Expedition of 1781," *Southern California Quarterly*, Vol. XV, Part I (November 1931).

Temple, Thomas Workman, "Se Fundaron un Pueblo de Espanoles, The Founding of Los Angeles." *Southern California Quarterly*, Vol. XV, Part I (November 1931).

Thompson, Jerry D. *Vaqueros in Blue and Gray.* Austin, Texas: Presidial Press, 1976.

Van Aken, Gertrude E. *El Pueblo Under the Spanish Flag.* Los Angeles, California: Los Angeles City Schools Publication No. 418, 1946.

Waldman, Carl. *Atlas of the North American Indian.* New York: Facts on File Publications, Inc., 1985.

Waldman, Carl. *Encyclopedia of Native American Tribes.* New York: Facts on File Publications, 1988.

Wasserman, Mark. *Everyday Life and Politics in Nineteenth Century Mexico: Men, Women, and War.* Albuquerque: The University of New Mexico Press, 2000.

Weber, Msgr. Francis J. (ed.). *Queen of the Missions: A Documentary History of Santa Barbara.* Hong Kong: Libra Press, Limited, 1979.

Whipperman, Bruce. *Pacific Mexico Handbook.* Chico, California: Moon Publications, Inc., 1997.

Whitehead, Robert S. *Citadel on the Channel: The Royal*

BIBLIOGRAPHY

Presidio of Santa Barbara: Its Founding and Construction, 1782-1798. Santa Barbara: Santa Barbara Trust for Historical Preservation, 1996.

Whitehead, Roy Elmer. *Lugo: A Chronicle of Early California.* Redlands, California: San Bernardino County Museum Association, 1978.

Williamson, Edwin. *The Penquin History of Latin America.* New York: Penguin Books, 1992.

Wilson, Barbara Juarez. *From Mission to Majesty: A Genealogy and History of Early California and Royal European Ancestors.* Baltimore, Maryland: Gateway Press, Inc., 1983.

Woods, Richard D. and Alvarez-Altman, Grace. *Spanish Surnames in the Southwestern United States: A Dictionary.* Boston, Massachusetts: G. K. Hall & Co., 1978.

INDEX

1740 REVOLT, 58-60
1850 FEDERAL CENSUS, 182
1860 FEDERAL CENSUS, 182-183 185
1870 FEDERAL CENSUS, 187-188
1880 FEDERAL CENSUS, 189
1900 FEDERAL CENSUS, 190 194
1910 FEDERAL CENSUS, 194
1920 FEDERAL CENSUS, 195
1ST CALIFORNIA NATIVE CAVALRY, 186
2ND DIVISION, 204
36TH TEXAS INFANTRY DIVISION, 203
79TH FIELD ARTILLERY, 206
9TH REGIMENT, 205
141ST REGIMENT, 203-204
158TH REGIMENTAL COMBAT TEAM, 203
200TH BATTALION, 202-203
515TH BATTALION, 202-203
ADAMS, John Quincy 179 Richard E 36
AGRICULTURE, 31-32
ALAMOS (SONORA), 65-66 68 71 102 104 106 133-136 141 143 145 161-163 184
ALTA CALIFORNIA, 4 72-73 75-78 80 84 86 91 95-99 101-108 110 117 144 167
ALVAREZ, Maria Bernarda 175
ANAUAC VALLEY, 40
ANAUAC VALLEY (MEXICO), 38-39
APACHE INDIANS, 60-63 65 82 86 145
APPLEBY, James Thomas 212 Nettie Jane, 212
ARAGON, Anna Maria de 142 Father Pedro Gabriel de 142
ARCHAIC PERIOD, 31
ARIZONA, 179 181
AYALA, Angela 199 David 191
AZTEC EMPIRE, 43-45
AZTEC INDIANS, 31 41-45 49
AZTLAN, 42

BAJA CALIFORNIA, 4 65 78 98-99 104 133 168 181
BAROYECA (SONORA), 161
BASULTO, Dora Melendez 48 136 143 153 197 199 209-212 Eusebio 48 136 143 153 210-212 214 Franceska Victoria Maria 210 Sarah Paz, 136 143 153 209-215
BATTLE OF BLOODY RIDGE, 204-205
BATTLE OF HEARTBREAK RIDGE, 205
BELLINDA HOSPITAL (SATICOY), 198
BERING LAND BRIDGE, 22
BERING SEA, 22-23
BERINGIA, 22
BERNABE, 59
BEVERLY HILLS (CALIFORNIA), 140
BOSQUE COUNTY (TEXAS), 212
BRINCKERHOFF SIDNEY B, 90
CABRILLO, Captain Juan Rodriguez 75 76
CAHITA LANGUAGE GROUP, 47 50-51 54-55
CALIFORNIA, Agriculture 99 American Citizenship 180-182 187 American Civil War 185-186 American Occupation 175 178-182 Cattle Industry 167 173 Civil War 185 186 Colonial Economy 167 Conquered 180 Culture 95 Economic Development 167 Foreign Commerce 167 170-173 Hispanic Population 139 154 176-178 Horse Population 172-173 Independence From Mexico 171-172 Indians 96-98 119 121-123 128-129 157-158 Mexican Economy 167 170-173 Mexican Period 167 171-181 Mexican-American War 179-182 Military posting 72-74 79-80 83-89 91-93 101-108 141-159 161 170 Missions 77-78 83-84 95-99 117-124 126

233

CALIFORNIA Missions (cont.)
130 141 145 147-148 150-151 156-157 161 170 Native Cavalry 186 Origin of Name 1 2 Presidios 78 84-86 97-98 117-131 137-139 141-159 161-165 168-171 Rights of Citizens 181-182 Settlement 95-99 101-115 117-130 133-135 137-138 Soldiers 70-73 89-93 97-98 115 117 122-130 137-139 141-159 161 168-171 175-178 Spanish Military Strategy 95-99 101-108 117-120 156-158 164 Statehood (1850), 182
CAMERO, Manuel 112
CAMPBELL, Leon 89 147
CARLOS III (King of Spain), 2 77-78 81-82 117 124
CARRIO, Rosa 163
CASTELO, Maria Gertrudis 135
CASTILLO, Pedro 80
CASTRO, Ana Geronima 161
CENTERVILLE (CALIFORNIA), 188
CHAPMAN, Charles E 5 151
CHICANO CULTURE, 215
CHIHUAHUA, 61-62
CHILE, 27
CHIRICAHUA INDIANS, 61
CHUMASH INDIANS, 123 128-129 157-158 193 218-219
CILLAS, Manual Theodoro 168 Maria Paula 168
CIVIL WAR, 185-186
CLIFTON (TEXAS), 212
COHN, Simon 188
COLON, Cristobal 27
COLONIAL INSTITUTIONS, 79-93
COLORADO, 181
COLORADO RIVER, 105
COLUMBUS, Christopher 27
COMANCHE INDIANS, 82 86
COMAPLA, Father Juan 187
COMPTON (CALIFORNIA), 192
CONFEDERATE STATES OF AMERICA, 185-186
CONTESTED EDEN, 180
CORDERO, Juan Maria 171
CORNERVILLE (CALIFORNIA), 188

CORONA, John 196
CORONADO, Francisco 66
CORTES, Hernan 34 45 75
COTTA, Josefade 163
CRY OF HIDALGO, 170
CULIACAN, 52 54 103
CULTURAL DIFFUSION, 26-28
CYCLES OF CONQUEST, 53
DAVIES, Nigel 33
DEEDS, Susan 58
DISEASE DEPOPULATION AND CULTURE CHANGE IN NORTHWESTERN NEW SPAIN 1518-1764, 52
EARLY DAYS OF SANTA BARBARA, 123
EL DORADO ELEMENTARY SCHOOL, 216
EL MUNI, 59
EL RIO (CALIFORNIA), 188 191-192
EL RIO CEMETERY, 191
ESPINOSA, Dorotea Barbara 106 143 148-152 167 184 219
ESQUIVEL, Apolinario 136 143 153 183 185-187 190 193 Eloise 185 Felix 190 Francesca 185 Maria 185 Ramona 185 Regina 136 143 153 187-192
ESQUIVEL FAMILY, 187-188
EUROPA MINE, 68
EVANS, Amanda Kate 214 Floyd Ray 214 Michael John 214
EXPEDITION OF 1769, 95-97
EXPEDITION OF 1781, 1-2 48 63 101-108 133-135 144 149 155-156 163 168 219
EZQUERR, Manuela Antonia 162
FAGES, Governor Pedro 166
FAULK, Odie B, 85-86 90
FELIZ, Anastasio Maria, 6 87 98 161-166 173 183-184 219 Captain Nicholas 161-162 Geronimo 161 Jose Vicente 162 164-166 Joseph 162 Juan Blas 161 Maria Antonia 143 173-174 176 183-184
FELIZ FAMILY, 66 161-166
FELIZ RANCHO, 166

FELIZ SURNAME, 161-162
FERNANDEZ, Antonio 158 Jose Rosalino 6 87 108 120 135-137 155-159 168 183-184 219 Maria Felipa 158 Maria Isabel 158 Maria Josefa 158 Maria Luciana 108 136 143 153 157-159 168-169 171 184 Maria Marcela 158
FERNANDEZ FAMILY, 66
FLORES, Lucy 195
FOWLER, Josephine 212-213
FRANCISCAN MISSIONARIES, 79-80 82 167
FRONTIER MILITARY ACTIVITY, 87-93 101-108 117-131 145 148-152 154 157-159
FUERTE (SINALOA), 66 70-71 136 155-156 184
GAINS, Father William A 192
GALVESTON (TEXAS), 212
GALVEZ, General Jose de 77
GARCIA, Celedonia 193 Soledad 193 Toribia 190
GERHARD, Peter 51-52 54 68
GILA RIVER, 105
GONZALEZ, Angela 197
GORALSA, Maria 134 148
GOYCOECHEA, Captain Felipe de 129-130 146 146 158
GRANADA HILLS HOSPITAL, 218
GRAND PRAIRIE (TEXAS), 212
GUERRA, Captain Antonio Maria Dela 186
GULF OF CALIFORNIA, 65
GUTIERREZ, Ramon A 180
GUZMAN, Diego 53 Nuno Beltran de 49 51-52
HAAS, Lisbeth 180
HAMILTON COUNTY (TEXAS), 212
HANCOCK, Major Henry 140
HANNA, Phil Townsend 106
HARLOW, Neil 180
HASINAI INDIAN CONFEDERACY, 82
HAWLEY, Walter A 123
HERNANDEZ, Frances 196 Leonardo 197 Marcos 197

HIDALGO, Father Miguel 170
HISPANIC, Culture 21 215 Heritage Month 206
HOLY CROSS HOSPITAL, 218
HOUSE OF OLIVAS, 125 172
HUBBERTEVA, 199
HUERTA, Captain Carlos C 206
HURDAIDE, Captain Diego de 54
ILLUSTRATED HISTORY OF MEXICAN LOS ANGELES, 1781-1985, 80
INDIANS CONVERSION, 79-84 128
INDIANS IN COLONIAL SOCIETY, 79-84 167
INDIANS MISSIONIZATION, 79-84 128
INDIGENOUS, History 21-28 Migrations 22-28
INSTITUTE OF ARCTIC AND ALPINE RESEARCH, 23
IRAPUATO (GUANAJUATO), 136 143 153 183
ITURBIDE, Emperor Agustin 171-172
JACKSON, Andrew 179
JALISCO, 48 51 133 218
JAPANESE IMPERIAL NAVY, 202
JESUIT MISSIONARIES, 56-59 66 79-84
JICARILLA INDIANS, 61
JIMENEZ, Carlos M 33
JONES, Bell Ross 212
KIOWA APACHE INDIANS, 61
KOREAN WAR, 201 204-206
KUNKEL, Albert Julius Max 212 Albert O 212 David Charles 136 143 153 212-213 215 Dennis James 213 Roland 212-213 Roland Lee 213 Tara Delarosa 213 215
KUNKEL FAMILY, 212
KUNKEL-VO, Jennifer 1 136 143 153 213 215 215-216 216-217 217-218 218-219 219
LAKE TEXCOCO, 43
LARA, Jose Fernanco de 111
LAS SERGAS DE ESPLANDIAN, 5
LASUEN, Father 84
LEON, Maria Margareta de 161-162

LIPAN APACHE INDIANS, 61
LORETO (BAJA CALIFORNIA), 98 104
LOS ANGELES, 1 87 96 101 109-115 117 133-137 147-148 150-151 155 158 164 Culture 215 Founding of 101-115 133-137 Humble beginnings 109 133 Indians 96-97 Pobladores 101-115 133-137 Racially Mixed Population 72-73 111-113 133 155
MACATHUR, General Douglas 202-203
MAGIC MOUNTAIN, 217
MAGYONA, Prisciliana 196
MAIZE, 32
MARTINEZ, Christina 195 Eddie 34 49 Fidele 190 Leonard 199 Mary 198 Willie 190
MAYA INDIANS, 31 36-37
MAYO INDIANS, 47 52-60 82
MEASLES, 52-53
MELENDEZ, Angela 198 Donald 198-199 204 Eva 198-199 Ignacio 197 Isabel Ortega 136 143 153 195 195-199 204 209 Jacoba 198-199 Raymundo 199 204 Refugio 136 143 153 197-199 204 209 Simon 198-199 204-206 209 Theodora 136 143 153 197-199
MENDES, Manuela 141 143
MESA ANTONIO, 112
MESCALERO INDIANS, 61
MESTIZAJE, 215
MEXICA INDIANS, 41-45
MEXICAN-AMERICAN WAR, 179-182
MEXICAN-AMERICANS, Military Contributions 185-186 201-207 Culture 215 Identity 48-49 187 201 Korean War Veterans 205 World War II Contribution 202-204 206-207
MEXICO, Agriculture 31-32 Area 33 Conquest 31 33-34 Epidemics 52-53 Frontier 71-73 73 75-93 Independence 170-172 Indigenous 31-45 47-63 Indigenous Languages

MEXICO Indigenous Languages (cont.)
33-34 37 Linguistic Diversity 33-37 49-50 Revolution 170-172 War with the United States 179-181
MEXICO CITY, 88 181
MIRANDA, Bernarda 142
MISSION HILLS (CALIFORNIA), 136 218
MISSIONS, 79-84 95
MISSIONS CALIFORNIA, 77-78 83-84 95-98 117-124 126 130 150 161
MIXTEC INDIANS, 31 36-37
MONROE, James 179
MONTEREY (CALIFORNIA), 77 84 99 120 144 149 163
MOORHEAD, Max L 93
MORENO, Jose 113
MOUNT HOLLY (NEW JERSEY), 214
NAHUATL, 41-42
NAVARRO, Jose Antonio 111
NAYARIT, 51
NEVADA, 181
NEVE FELIPE DE, 98-99 101 118 124 133 137
NEW JERUSALEM (CALIFORNIA), 188-190
NEW MEXICO, 82-83 179 181
NEWHALL (CALIFORNIA), 213
NEWTON, Linda 27
NORTH AMERICA, 23-28 31
NORTH FRONTIER OF NEW SPAIN, 51
NORTH HOLLYWOOD (CALIFORNIA), 213
NUEVA VIZCAYA, 54 65
OAXACA, 36-37
OLIVA VISTA MIDDLE SCHOOL, 216
OLIVAS, Apolinario Guillermo 177 Blas Felipe 177 Carolina 182 Carolina Celestina 177 Cosme 152 Felipe 182 Francisco 148 153 Guillermo 182 Isabel 182 Jose de Los Santos 177 182 Jose Dolores 136 143 152-153 169 171 175-178 182-184 Jose Ignacio Antonio 177

OLIVAS (cont.)
  Jose Maria 177 Jose Pablo 106 136 143 149 152-153 167-171 176 184 219 Jose Santiago 177 Jose Victoriana 182 186 Juan de Dios 150 Juan Matias 6 87 106 108 120 148-155 167-168 183-184 219 Juana 152 177 182 Juana de Dios 177 Madeline 152 Maria 152 Maria Antonia 136 143 153 174 177 182-184 187 Maria Eulalia 177 Maria Nicolasa 106 149 152 Mariana Silveria 177 Nicolas Mado 177 Ramona 182 Susanna 174 177-178 182
OLIVAS FAMILY, 66
OLMEC INDIANS, 36
OPATA INDIANS, 82
OPERATION DESERT SHIELD, 206
OPERATION DESERT STORM, 206
ORRANTE, Paz 195
ORSI, Richard J 180
ORTEGA, Barbara 194 Carrie 190 Christina 195 Clara 190 Dionisio 189 Felix V 195 Genevive 189 Gregorio 136 143 153 187-194 209 Isabel 136 143 153 190 195-199 204 209 John 190 Jose 190 Lieutenant Jose Francisco 118-123 127-129 Luciano 195 Lucy 190 Luz 195 Marcelina 189 Maria 189 Maria L 189 Michaela 189 Nevis 194 Paz 195 Solomon 188-189 Sonjie 195 Thomas 190 Valentine 136 143 153 189-196 209
ORTEGA FAMILY, 187-199
OXNARD (CALIFORNIA), 192-199
PACOIMA COMMUNITY HOSPITAL, 199
PAPAGOS INDIANS, 82
PARRA, Antonio Maria 146 Francisco Xavier 142 144 Maria Dolores 106 143-147 173 184 219 Nicolas Alberto 142
PARRA FAMILY, 66
PEARL HARBOR ATTACK, 202
PENJAMO (GUANAJUATO), 136 143 197

PEREZ, Jobie 199
PHELAN, Rachel 110
PHILIPPINE ISLANDS, 202-203
PIERCE COLLEGE, 213
PIMA INDIANS, 65 82
PIOUS FUND, 82
POBLADORES, 101-115 133-137
POLK, James Knox 178-180
PORTOLA, Gaspar de 77-78 96
PRESIDIOS, California 78 84-86 97-98 141-159 161 168-171 Frontier 79-80 84-88
PUEBLO INDIANS, 82-83
PUEBLOS, 79-81 86-87 99
PURISIMA CONCEPCION MISSION, 117 127 130 151
QUEEN OF THE MISSIONS, 118
QUIJADA, Juan Ataxia 163 Maria Rita 162-163 Vicente 163
QUINTERO, Catharina 135 Fabiana 135 Jose Clemente 135 138 Luis 6 108 112 133-140 146 211 215 219 Maria Concepcion 108 Maria Juana Josefa 108 135-136 158 168 184 219 Maria Tomasa 135 Sebastiana 139-140
QUINTERO FAMILY, 66 112-113 115 134-140
QUINTERO SURNAME, 134
RADDING, Dr Cynthia 60
RANCHERIA PEOPLE, 53-54
RANCHO LOS FELIZ, 166
REFF, Daniel T 52
RENO (NEVADA), 214
RIO GRANDE BOUNDARY, 179
RIOS-BUSTMANATE, Dr Antonio 72 80
RIVERA, Captain Fernando 101-108 144-145 149
RODEO DE LA AGUAS, 140
RODRÌGUEZ, Joaquin 135 137 Pablo 112
ROMERO, Isabela 161
ROSA, Casimiro Dela 209-210 Refugio Dela 209
ROSARIO (SINALOA), 66 69-70 106 136 143 148-149 167 184
ROSAS, Alejandro 112 Basilio 111

RUBIO, Maria Petra 133-138 219
SACRED HEART CHURCH, 196
SAIGON (VIETNAM), 136 216
SAN BLAS (NAYARIT), 84 86 98-99 158 169
SAN BUENAVENTURA, 188-189
SAN BUENAVENTURA MISSION, 117 121-122 127 130 138 157-158 164 187 190 192
SAN DIEGO, Indians 97-98 Military Strategy 95-99 Mission 97 Presidio 84 95-98 119-120 145-147 150 162 174
SAN FERNANDO VALLEY, 209 214-215 218
SAN FRANCISCO, 84
SAN GABRIEL MISSION, 97 105-106 108-109 117 136-137 143 145 147-148 151 155-157 162 168 173
SAN LUIS OBISPO MISSION, 127 130
SAN MIGUEL DE CULIACAN, 52
SANDOVAL, Cleofas 196-197 Gregory 197 199 Leonidas 196 Maria Louisa 197 Valentine 196-197 199
SANTA BARBARA, 84 114 117-131 136-138 143 145-146 150-154 157-158 163-165 Expedition 117-123 137-138 Founding 117-128 Military Life 117 123-131 147-152 154 157-159 164-165 168-169 173-176 Mission 117-124 126 130 150 168-169 Population 128 130 139 152 168-169 176 Presidio 2 114-115 118-131 137-138 145-147 150-152 154 157-159 163-165 168-169 172 178 Presidio Census 127-128 130 138 146 150-151 157-158 164-165 168-169 176-178 Racial Mixture, 127-128 130 138 146-147 149 152 158
SANTA BARBARA ROYAL RANCHO, 127
SANTA BARBARA COUNTY, 182 185
SANTA CLARA CEMETERY, 195-196 199 209

SANTA CLARA CHURCH, 191
SANTA PAULA (CALIFORNIA), 136 143 196
SANTA YNES MISSION, 117 130 176
SATICOY (CALIFORNIA), 136 143 153 195 198-199 204 209
SERI INDIANS, 65
SERRA, Father Junipero 77-78 83-84 120-121 123-124 126 128 137
SHIVE (TEXAS), 212
SIBERIA, 22
SIMI VALLEY (CALIFORNIA), 209
SINALOA, 1-2 47-63 65-73 82 87 101-105 133 148-149 161-162
SINALOA EMIGRATION, 66 71-73
SINALOA INDIAN REBELLIONS, 51-59
SINALOA MILITARY OPPORTUNITIES, 71-73
SINALOA RACIALLY MIXED POPULATION, 70-73
SINALOA SOCIAL STRATIFICATION, 71-73
SLIDELL, John 179
SMALLPOX, 52-53 104 168
SMITH, Professor Michael E 42-43
SMITHSONIAN INSTITUTE, 28
SOLDADOS DE CUERA, 2 87-93 96 101-108 134-135 137 141-159 161 164 168-169 171 173-176 183
SONORA, 1-2 47-63 65-74 82 87 101-106 133 142 144-145 161 Emigration 66 71-73 Indian Rebellions 51-63 Miltiary Opportunities 71-73 Racially Mixed Population 70-73 Social Stratification 71-73
SOUTH AMERICA, 27
SPAIN, Colonial Institutions 79-93 Military 72-73 87-93 Military Expenditures 81-83 Racial Classifications 113
SPANISH ARMADA, 76
SPANISH EMPIRE, 1 5-6 31 44 47-63 65-66 75-87 101 106-108
SPANISH MILITARY WEAPONS, 92-93

SPICER, Edward H 53
STEVENS, Meredith 114 125 172
SYLMAR (CALIFORNIA), 212-213 216-217
TABASCO, 36
TAPIA, Francesca 193 Juan 193 Lucia 193 Maria A 193 Theodora 136 143 153 192-196
TAPIA FAMILY, 192-193 218
TAPIA-GARCIA, Maria Marta 193 196
TARASCAN INDIANS, 31 49
TAYLOR, Zachary 179
TEHUACAN, 32
TENOCHTITLAN, 43-45 75
TEOTIHUACAN, 39-40
TEXAS, 178-180
TIERRA DEL FUEGO, 27
TLAXCALAN INDIANS, 49
TOLTEC INDIANS, 31 41
TOURING TOPICS, 106
TREATY OF CAHUENGA, 180
TREATY OF CORDOVA, 170
TREATY OF GUADALUPE HIDALGO, 181-182
TUBAC, 162
VALDES, Antonio Maria 139 Basilio 139 Eugenio 135 137 139-140 Joaquin 183 Josepha 183 Maria 139 Maria Rita Quiteria 140
VALENCIA (CALIFORNIA), 217
VALENZUELA, Antonio Maria 143 173-174 184 Baltasar 174 Clemente 141-143 Estanislao 147 Francisco Xavier 162 Gertrudis 174 Jose 176 Maria Gertrudis 136 143 153 162-166 176 181-184 219 Maria Trinidad 174 Pedro Gabriel 6 87 106 108 120 141-148 173 183-184 219 Vicente Antonio 147-148
VALENZUELA FAMILY, 66
VALLEY COLLEGE, 214
VALLEY OF MEXICO, 38-40
VAN DELLEN, Katherine 188
VAN NUYS (CALIFORNIA), 216
VANEGAS, Cosme 175 Jose 112

VAQUEROS IN BLUE AND GRAY, 185
VASQUEZ, Mary Lou 199
VEGA, Maria Gabriela de la 142 144
VENTURA (CALIFORNIA), 188-189 198-199
VENTURA CITY COLLEGE, 204
VENTURA COUNTY (CALIFORNIA), 182 194 209
VENTURA JUNIOR HIGH SCHOOL, 204
VERACRUZ, 36
VIETNAM, 136 216
VIETNAM WAR, 206
VIETNAM WAR HISPANIC INVOLEMENT, 206
VILLA VICENTE FERRER, 140
VILLA SINALOA (SINALOA), 162
VILLAVICENCIO ANTONIO CLEMENTE, 112
VO, James 136 143 153 216-217 Jessica Saramai 135-136 143 153 218-219 Ryan 135-136 143 153 218-219
WAINWRIGHT, General Jonathan 203
WEBER, Monsignor Francis J 118
WILSON, Benjamin 140
WOODLAND HILLS (CALIFORNIA), 213
WORLD WAR II, 48 202-204
YAQUI INDIANS, 47 51-59 82
YUMA INDIANS, 105 156
ZAPOTEC INDIANS, 31 36-37
ZUNIGA, Lieutenant Jose 104 145

About the Authors

Jennifer Vo is an eleventh-generation Californian through her ancestor Luis Quinter, who was one of the original settlers of Los Angeles in 1781. Along with other members of her family, she has taken an interest in her Chumash Indian roots and is involved in some of their activities. Ms. Vo was born and raised in Southern California and is employed as a senior editor for a Los Angeles publishing company. She is married with two children.

John Schmal is a native of Hermosa Beach, California. He is a genealogist and historian, specializing in Mexican lineages. He previously co-authored "Mexican-American Genealogical Research: Following the Paper Trail to Mexico" with Donna S. Morales. Mr. Schmal and a friend are collaborating on a manuscript in progress relating to Indigenous Mexican history and statistics.

Mr. Schmal belongs to the Association of Professional Genealogists, Familia, and the Genealogy Society of Hispanic America. He is also a board member of the Society for Hispanic Historical and Ancestral Research (SHHAR) and is an associate editor and indexer of SHHAR's newsletter, www.somosprimos.com. Mr Schmal works for a publishing company in Los Angeles, California.

www.ingramcontent.com/pod-product-compliance
Lightning Source LLC
Chambersburg PA
CBHW070641160426
43194CB00009B/1530